Choices

Choices

God's and Ours

Paul Shotsberger

FOREWORD BY
Robert Black

RESOURCE *Publications* • Eugene, Oregon

CHOICES
God's and Ours

Resource Publications
An Imprint of Wipf and Stock Publishers
199 W. 8th Ave., Suite 3
Eugene, OR 97401

www.wipfandstock.com

PAPERBACK ISBN: 978-1-5326-4459-7
HARDCOVER ISBN: 978-1-5326-4460-3
EBOOK ISBN: 978-1-5326-4461-0

Manufactured in the U.S.A.

To my wife Susan and the people of Ukraine,
thank you for choosing me.

Contents

Foreword

In *The Art of Virtue,* Benjamin Franklin wrote, "We stand at the crossroads, each minute, each hour, each day, making choices." He was right, of course. Our lives are the sum total of our choices. But Franklin continued, "Each choice is made in the context of whatever value system we have selected to govern our lives. In selecting that value system, we are, in a very real way, making the most important choice we will ever make."

Any value system which isn't centered on God is out of sync with the very one who made our choices possible. Our creation in His image means that, like Him, we are endowed with intellect, emotion, and will. As a result, we are able to do the three things essential to personhood – we are able to think, to feel, and to choose.

Our Maker has chosen to let us choose.

It almost sounds like a paradox: *The infinite God has a plan for us, and finite human beings are free to make choices.* In fact, both halves of the statement are true! As for how that works with fallible folks in the give and take of everyday life, the answer all too often is not very well.

Sometimes we're far too casual about the impact of the choices we make, and life-altering decisions are made without careful consideration. Let's be honest. We can be impulsive, forgetting that actions have consequences. (Like you, I'm mentally inserting memories of my own personal fumbles here.)

On the other hand, some of us fret unnecessarily over relatively inconsequential decisions. A classmate of mine from long ago is a case in point. He was determined to find and follow God's will for His life, but for him, that very worthy desire translated into seeking guidance not only on life's biggest decisions but also on the smallest. When he took forever to pass through the cafeteria line one day, I asked him why. In all seriousness he replied that he was asking God whether he should take the ham or the chicken, the beans or the peas, the biscuit or the cornbread. Multiply that burden by the countless choices a college student has to make every day, and you can imagine the stress he was under. He dropped out just a few weeks into the semester.

Granted, that's an extreme case, but it's not unusual to find Christians struggling in less spectacular ways to align their choices with God's will . . . putting out fleeces, over-analyzing circumstances, wondering if a random occurrence is really a divine message in disguise.

I hope they read this book. I wish my classmate could have read it.

My friend and faculty colleague Paul Shotsberger has masterfully explored the relationship between God's desires and our decisions. The biblical examples he marshals shed revealing light on the interplay between creature and Creator when we're in the throes of difficult decision-making.

Choices is a great book to read at the crossroads Ben Franklin was talking about. I for one am glad I chose to read it.

Robert Black, Ph.D.
Professor Emeritus of Religion
Southern Wesleyan University

Preface

THIS BOOK REPRESENTS MUSINGS of mine from the last fifteen years: in some cases actual teachings, in others just random writings. I didn't think they particularly had anything to do with each other until God showed me the theme of choices running throughout. Once informed of this thread, it's hard to see them any other way. Perhaps my main motivation in writing about choices, God's and ours, is my rather diversified denominational upbringing and subsequent church memberships. I was brought up Baptist and Christian and Missionary Alliance, but became part of Presbyterian congregations in early adulthood, including being a deacon and elder in the Evangelical Presbyterian Church. This latter experience gave me a deep exposure to the principles of determinism and pre-destination (God's choice). Then came Ukraine. While an elder in a Presbyterian church, my wife and I were invited to spend a year in Ukraine as advisors for a relatively young network of Russian-speaking Bible schools. I took a leave of absence from my university to accept the invitation, but half way through our time there, unexpectedly, I became director of the network. One year became two became seven. In that time, I was working primarily with Pentecostal and Charismatic churches, and so it was that I was given an education in the essential role of free will in the believer's life (our choice). Since returning from Ukraine, I have been a professor at a Wesleyan university where I have had the opportunity to delve into the theology of John Wesley, all the while being part of a non-denominational church.

So, I am a bit of a mashup theologically, which perhaps makes me more suited to writing a book such as the one you are reading. The book is intended as practical theology that can inform not only ways of thinking but also ways of doing. The biblical characters in this book are my dear friends who have taught me much over the years. I hope you come to love them as much as I do.

Introduction

I served in the United States Navy for sixteen years, four years active and twelve years reserve. While on active duty, I served on an amphibious ship under three different captains. One thing you quickly learn onboard ship is that the captain rules with an iron hand—a Navy ship is probably the closest thing to a monarchy that we have in the United States. The ship is literally the captain's kingdom, especially at sea. The captain has a sovereign will for the ship to get from point A to point B, while also successfully participating in exercises or activities that have been assigned. In Greek this is known as the captain's *boulema*, his or her pre-set plan. The Captain also has certain desires, chief among them being that everyone in the crew safely and productively contributes to the successful completion of the mission. And, these wishes are expressed in the rules and regulations governing the crew's behavior included on the many placards containing instructions and warnings posted throughout the ship. In Greek this is the *thelema* of the captain, his or her desire. Why desire? Because our technology has not yet advanced to the point that the work of an entire ship can be automated.

So, there is another dynamic at play, and it is the choices the crew makes every day the ship is at sea. Individuals in the crew each make decisions all day long that affect their own well-being. Let's call this moral will. Most of the crew are careful in their jobs and are obedient to the warning signs around them. However, ships are inherently dangerous places, and either due to negligence or disobedience, every once in a while someone gets hurt. I have been witness to horrific accidents and have myself been involved in some unfortunate incidents. I can tell you that it doesn't take much to endanger the crew on a ship at sea. A step may be skipped in the process of repairing a piece of large and powerful machinery which when turned back on reacts violently and unexpectedly, injuring whoever is nearby; a box or container may be lazily and only partially secured against the effects of rough seas and coming loose careens into an individual; a stage or safety line may be only loosely secured and so not be able to hold the weight of the person it is supposed to protect, who then comes crashing down to the deck of the ship from four stories above.

As a result of the moral will of the crew members, the injured person or persons have to spend the rest of the voyage recovering from their misadventures. The ship will still complete its mission and arrive at its destination, so the captain's *boulema* will be realized. But the captain's *thelema* will not be accomplished for everyone because members of the crew have not been able to contribute to the success of the voyage. So, as much as the ship is the captain's kingdom, it is nonetheless a complex and dangerous place where almost anything can happen.

This is not unlike the kingdom of God. There is God's sovereign *boulema* that is certain to be achieved—the ultimate success of the Gospel, the ultimate defeat of evil. I mean, just read Revelation. We know how the story ends, and we know God wins. So, the ship will arrive at its destination and its mission, that " . . . the earth will be filled with the knowledge of the glory of the Lord as the waters cover the sea" (Hab 2:14) will be accomplished. We also see over and over in Scripture God's *thelema* for his people, expressed primarily in his commandments which are intended to bless and protect his followers. But then there is that nasty business of the believer's moral will, the thing that can lend itself to the accomplishment of the *boulema*, but just as easily can work against the *thelema* and mess everything up. Have you ever wondered why moral will even exists? Why do we have choices anyway? They just seem to get in the way and make everything messy in the kingdom. Yet, our moral will is part of God's plan, just as much as his *boulema* and *thelema.*

But, that's not the whole story. As we will see in the coming pages, even after God has made his choices and set events in motion, sometimes he chooses to disrupt his own system and intervene in the affairs of humans in order to accomplish some particular purpose, often in unexpected ways that on their face can seem unfair. So, as the saying goes, it's complicated. This book does not so much diagnose the choices made by either God or people as it does just tell stories, mostly from the Bible. No effort is made to gloss over the messiness because I believe that messiness is an inherent characteristic of the kingdom of God here on earth. Yet we need to appreciate the gravity of both God's choices and our own. There are consequences. To the extent that we are conscious of the choices being made and mindful of the effects of those choices, we will be in that part of the crew that is on mission, that brings glory to our Captain, and at the end of the voyage hears the Captain say to each of us, " . . . 'Well done, good and faithful servant! . . . '" (Matt 25:21). So, here is the thesis of this book, to be tested by the reader in the following chapters: the highest *boulema* is God's purpose to bring about maximum glory for himself, the purest *thelema* is God's desire to bless and protect his people, and the most powerful moral will is our agreement with God's *boulema* and *thelema.* "Do not conform any longer to the pattern of this world, but be transformed by the renewing of your mind. Then you will be able to test and approve what God's will is—his good, pleasing and perfect will" (Rom 12:2). It's all about choices.

Chapter 1

The Choices God Makes

God's natural laws that he has established, the physical laws that govern the universe, help us understand theologically how and when God intervenes in human affairs. I am a mathematician, so I will use probability as an example, but I promise not to test the reader's patience with this analogy. I have no reason to doubt that the laws of probability were established at creation, much as gravity and other physical laws. God set this amazing system in place as background for our lives, parameters if you will for living on earth. Like it or not, these laws exist and cannot be broken by us. Further, these systems are connected to each other; results in one system are confirmed in another, such as the connection between mathematical laws and scientific laws. It's all quite complex and beautiful and, above all for the mathematician, it produces results that do not contradict themselves.

Now, consider the question: if God put this complex and beautiful system in place to govern life on this earth, does it make sense that God would then oversee and in fact determine every roll of the dice, every card pulled from a deck, every twirl of some spinner? What's the point? The system ensures predictable outcomes for large numbers of events. In other words, the system works. Why would God need to be in every event or experiment? He wouldn't unless, of course, he had some specific reason for that intervention: unless for some reason he wanted to circumvent the laws he himself had established in order to serve some greater purpose.

The most direct example of this principle would be when lots were cast in the Old and New Testament. For instance, we are told in 1 Samuel 10 that Samuel the priest had already anointed Saul as the first king of Israel, but then in front of the entire nation he chose lots from all the tribes, and through this random-seeming selection process wound up identifying Saul from among all the people. The odds of this happening would have been astronomical but for God's choice to intervene. We can also think about times when God countermanded the physical laws of the universe to accomplish his *boulema*. The two most obvious examples are when the Sun stood still in the sky for Joshua (Joshua 10) and when the shadow on the steps moved backward for Hezekiah (Isaiah 38). In these cases, there was an intervention into the system of the motion of the Earth around the Sun (and many other related laws) in order to create a specific sign for God's people. Likewise, if we think of weather as a system that God established at creation, which has predictable outcomes over long periods of time, God chose to intervene during a storm on the Sea of Galilee as a sign for the disciples of Jesus (Mark 4:35–41).

Can God circumvent the laws he himself has established in order to accomplish his *boulema*? Yes, of course. Does he do it on a regular basis? It seems not. Are some events in God's universe pre-determined? It seems so. We see this in Acts 4:27–28, where the believers pray, "Indeed Herod and Pontius Pilate met together with the Gentiles and people of Israel in this city to conspire against your holy servant Jesus, whom you anointed. They did what your power and will had decided beforehand should happen." Well then, are all events pre-determined? We can answer that question with another question: Why would they be? Why would God establish these incredibly complex, powerful, and coherent systems if he only ever intended to determine the outcomes, event by event? It doesn't really make much sense.

Now, here's the theological application: Just as God has established physical laws for governing the universe, he has also established spiritual laws. Perhaps the most pervasive biblical law is the principle of sowing and reaping. God expects us to sow righteousness, and when we do, we reap spiritual blessing. When we do not, we suffer. This was the basis of God's covenant with Israel. Biblically, it's a very straight-forward principle with few exceptions. Yet, there are exceptions. There are those whose lives were anything but models of sowing in righteousness, and yet God's blessing was upon them. How else can we explain the outcome of Jacob's life? God simply chose, for his own reasons, to set aside the law of sowing and reaping and blessed Jacob and his family. God did this in order to establish the nation of Israel and eventually lead them into the Promised Land. In other words, God had a higher purpose than even the spiritual law he himself had established.

Speaking now of the historical events necessary for his mission to be accomplished, I believe God's *boulema* applies at all times and in every case. In other words, the system works. There is no need to pre-determine each outcome, similar to the roll of the dice in probability. But I also believe that God does, from time to time, choose to intervene in the system, to change some particular outcome to achieve maximum glory for himself. It's hard to read the Bible any other way. It seems, in fact, that God delights in doing this, in making the last first and the first last, because it directly points to him as the source of all blessing. I call these interventions God's "deep selects." In the military, there is a pecking order for promotion, an established order of rank and priority among officers. When a position of authority comes open, higher-ups go to the list, and it is immediately obvious who is next in line for the job. The system works and there are few exceptions. However, there *are* exceptions. In specific circumstances and for particular reasons, it is decided to pass over those at the top of the list for someone farther down. This happened at the beginning of World War II when Chester Nimitz was chosen to be Commander in Chief of the Pacific Fleet. He was not only a more junior officer, he was also a submariner—a highly unlikely choice.[1] And yet, the decision was made, and the United States military effort in the Pacific profited as a result.

1. See for example Knortz, "The Strategic Leadership of Chester W. Nimitz"

We see God involved in this "deep select" process at very strategic points in the biblical account, choosing Joseph over his brothers, David over his brothers, Gideon the nobody farmer from the nothing family, the teenager Mary from the tiny village of Nazareth, fishermen, a tax collector, and the Christian-hater Saul. Though some had questions for God about why they were chosen, we get the sense that their acceptance of God's proposal was never in doubt. In other words, God had determined the outcome. Despite having a system in place for blessing individuals, God chose to lay aside the system in order to bless beyond the individual, to bless the nations.

Though we might be able to talk ourselves into accepting this aspect of God's sovereignty, unfortunately, it only opens the door for more theological difficulties. The hard reality of the way in which God chooses to bless is that, as with games based on probability, if someone wins that invariably means someone else loses. Biblically, we might say that where there is choosing there is also losing. The choice of Jacob resulted in the loss of birthright and blessing on Esau's part; the choice of Joseph resulted in his brothers bowing down to him in homage; the honoring of Job at the end of his story resulted in the humiliation of his friends. As difficult as the outcome was for those who lost in these situations, we are comforted by the fact that ultimately there was redemption available for the "losers." In each of the above cases, God had made provision for those on the short end of the stick through the one who was blessed.

But this was not the case for all of those in the Bible who lost out on God's blessing. For some, redemption never came. God hardened Pharaoh's heart in order to bless the Israelites, and as far as we know, that condition did not change. Esther won the king's favor and salvation for her people, but as a direct result, Haman swung on the gallows. Jesus called Judas Iscariot " . . . the one doomed to destruction . . . " (John 17:12), and Judas committed suicide having never rid himself of that label. These figures, Pharaoh, Haman, and Judas Iscariot, were pivotal in God's plan of blessing for the nations. In each case, God intervened in the affairs of the human race to bring about a particular outcome that would glorify himself, which is completely within his purview as maker of the universe. And though we cheer for the winners (which includes us) in each of these situations, we are sobered by the tragedy that resulted for the losers. We hear echoes of this reality in God's promise to the nation of Israel recorded in Isa 43:4: "Since you are precious and honored in my sight, and because I love you, I will give people in exchange for you, nations in exchange for your life."

Why does God do this sort of thing? Why would he establish a perfectly good system and then simply set it aside? Further, when does he choose to do such a thing? Under what circumstances? The story of Jesus raising Lazarus from the dead in John 11 is instructive here. What more pervasive and enduring physical system can we imagine on this earth than the birth and death cycle? We are born, we live, we get sick, and we die. However, even though this was the reality for the vast majority of those whose stories are written about in the Bible, it was not true for everyone—time to time, the story would continue. This happened in both the Old Testament and New Testament. But among those stories, the account of Jesus' resurrection of Lazarus stands out because of the deliberate choices Jesus, God himself, made.

The key decision made by Jesus was the one to stay on where he was for an additional two days after receiving the news that Lazarus was ill. Jesus' choice resulted in two pivotal events: The death of Lazarus prior to Jesus' arrival in Bethany, and Lazarus having been in the tomb four days before Jesus came on the scene. For Lazarus's friends and family, it was game, set, and match. When Jesus finally arrived at their little town, both Martha and Mary expressed their understanding of God's system by saying, "LORD, if you had been here, my brother would not have died" (vss 21, 32). This statement says, essentially, "I understand the system: people who are sick can get better, but not people who have died. You should have gotten here earlier." However, Martha added a note of hope that Mary did not: "But I know that even now God will give you whatever you ask" (vs 22). In other words, God still makes his choices. A theological debate ensued between Jesus and

Martha during which they discussed weighty topics like the resurrection of the dead and who Jesus really is. It seems clear from Martha's answers to Jesus' questions that her thoughts were on the hereafter, rather than the moment. This contrasts with Mary's mindset, which was totally focused on the present.

When we ask why God chooses to intervene in his own system, we have to be mindful of this particular story from the Bible. God has his reasons, and God makes his choices, but those choices are made with us in mind. This is a remarkable but undeniable fact of Scripture. Somehow, God's *boulema* is molded around our fragile existence. How else can we explain Jesus' response to Mary? Whereas Martha made her statement to Jesus concerning her brother while standing at eye level in front of him, Mary makes the same statement from the dirt at Jesus' feet. Jesus went to Bethany with the express purpose of raising Lazarus from the dead, primarily because it would bring maximum glory to his Father. When he arrived at that town, he was the only one who knew that in just a few minutes Lazarus would be alive once again. Yet, with Mary at his feet, he began to cry. The crowd around him said, "See how he loved him" (vs 36), and that was certainly true. But clearly, Jesus was not grieving.

I believe Jesus' tears are unexplainable apart from the fact that Mary had found a way to touch his heart. She was someone who had spent time at Jesus' feet while he was teaching, and she was affirmed by Jesus as having chosen the "better" way. She would be at his feet again when she anointed them with perfume prior to his death, a deeply significant act that Jesus said was his preparation for burial. We must always remember that God's choices are not made in an eternal vacuum, devoid of any concern for his people. This is as true of the Old Testament as the New. How else can we understand the strange conversation between Abraham and God over the fate of the inhabitants of Sodom (Gen 18:16–33)? Or Moses pleading with God to spare the Israelites after the debacle of the golden calf, which resulted in the unimaginable: God altering a decision he had made (Exod 32:9–14). Or God's accolades for Moses and Samuel in Jer 15:1, and Noah, Daniel and Job in

Ezek 14:14—those who could touch his heart with their intercession. God's pre-eminent concern is for his glory, but it seems in choosing that which will glorify him, he leaves the door of intercession ajar for those righteous ones who are *also* his glory.

This brings us to the ultimate choice: salvation. Is there a theological debate that has divided more Christians, churches and denominations throughout church history? Whose choice is it? Is it God's or the individual's? Of course, in one sense, it's all God's choice because he set up the system of salvation in the first place. If we apply the principles from the preceding discussion, we may conclude that God established a system that works wherein individuals, without the need for some kind of prior approval, are free to come to God through Christ Jesus and receive forgiveness for their sins and reconciliation with God. However, God reserves the right to intervene in this system, from time to time, to produce a salvation that goes far beyond the individual. If we give it a minute's thought, all of us can come up with an example of a salvation story we are familiar with (perhaps even our own) that is so unlikely it defies human logic. The person was not "on the road to salvation." In fact, it was quite the opposite—the person actually was an active condemner of God and of his followers. Yet, God in his mercy and for his glory "deep selected" that individual to be a part of his Kingdom.

Let's consider a less controversial but equally mysterious choice, one we are called on to make every day as Christians: being led by the Spirit. In Romans 8, the Apostle Paul writes extensively on this subject, presenting us with a choice for living. We are either led by the Spirit, or we are led by our sinful nature, he says. It is our choice, but there are only two options, much as when Moses presented the Israelites with the choice of life or death, encouraging them to choose life. What exactly does Paul mean by being "led by the Spirit"? Interpretations abound, but here's my best effort at a definition: We are led by the Spirit when we do the right thing for the right reason at the right time. It is not simply a matter of doing the right thing, or even doing the right thing for the right reason.

Many philosophers extol the virtues of acting morally, based on moral principles, but most of them do not care a bit about being obedient to God. Following the Spirit's leading means going with his timing, trusting his order, intent and outcome are the best we could hope for in this life. We are not simply reasoning our way through each day, trying to choose from the best that our human nature has to offer. According to the Apostle Paul, our human nature is in direct opposition to the way of the Holy Spirit because our human nature is by definition sinful. This sinful nature of ours is prone to skepticism and motivated by self-protection, and so the last thing (on our own) we would choose for ourselves would be complete dependence on someone else, even if that Someone was infinitely wise and loving. Our human nature can convince us that God is not interested in our personal needs, that it's all about Kingdom work, and we are expected to sacrifice everything we feel and all of our needs for that work.

When we give ourselves over to being led by the Spirit, however, we discover that God is intensely interested in us, personally, and he is more than willing to take care of our needs. But, he also knows the *time* to meet those needs, and timing in the Kingdom of God is everything. The ideal of living a moral life is then subsumed into the reality of being Spirit-led. Is it possible to do the right thing for the right reason at the right time and not have it be moral? I'm not sure I could come up with an example of that. The difference between being led by the Spirit and trying to live a moral life is that instead of looking for a one-size-fits-all approach to life that is based solely on principle, we flexibly follow the Spirit who is infinitely good and yet also infinitely creative. *That* is a life worth living.

What about God's choice in all of this? Similar to salvation, God has established a system whereby we can be led by his Spirit. This is his *thelema* for us, his best offer. The question is simply whether we will choose the way he has made for us. Further, once we decide to be Spirit-led—a decision that takes place daily—from that point until we decide otherwise, we are giving God free reign to make choices for us. This is similar to the illustration of the captain and his crew mentioned in the Introduction. When a crewmember complies with the captain's intention and desire, that crewmember's moral will is subsumed in the captain's *boulema* and *thelema*. When we agree with God's *boulema* and *thelema*, a spiritual Venturi Effect takes over, and we are drawn into his amazing plan for bringing his Kingdom to this earth. Our choice is consumed by, and becomes indistinguishable from, his choice.

What happens when we do not opt for the Spirit's leading, in particular, the Spirit's timing? We can wind up as the non-contributing crewmember of the captain's ship, not a part of his *boulema* and *thelema*, separated from his presence and satisfaction. We become like the woman in Song of Songs chapter 5 who initially refused to open the door to her lover, complaining of having to get out of bed and get her feet dirty all over again. Eventually, she pulls herself out of the bed, but when she goes to the door, he is no longer there. This is a tragic story that hits close to home for most Christians. Many times we know the right thing to do, but we believe that we can respond to God at our convenience. As a result, we miss out on the God-encounter that was intended for us.

And this brings me to the subject of the significance of our choices. Whether it is salvation, or being led by the Spirit, or any other choice that we make, what is it that we are choosing? And why do our choices matter to God? Some would say that we have no choices, that everything is pre-determined because God is sovereign; he knows what he's doing and we don't. Some think that every choice God gives us is a test of some kind. Put in negative terms, every choice is an opportunity for God to teach us a lesson, to show us just how short of the mark we fall, to remind us who's boss. Some think life is really all about our choices, that God has somehow limited himself in such a way that he can't intervene in human affairs. So, he sits up in heaven wringing his hands, hoping we make the right decisions. It should be apparent from the preceding arguments that I don't find any of these explanations very satisfying.

As with most spiritual principles, I tend to choose the simplest, most straight-forward explanation possible, one that I believe reflects the heart of the Creator while not denying reality. So, here's why I think God values our choices: because his *thelema* is to bless us. Yes, he puts (at least) two options in front of us and asks us to choose, but what he's really looking for is an excuse to bless us. In fact, I believe that life is just a series of offers from God for blessing. It is a sign of our depravity as sinful humans that we can interpret God's offer as some sort of trial or burden to endure. God places someone in our path who needs to hear the Gospel, or he invites us to the mission field, or he . . . (you fill in the blank). He intends to bless us, but we see it as an inconvenience. We respond like the woman in Song 5:3, "I have taken off my robe—must I put it on again? I have washed my feet—must I soil them again?" How profoundly sad. The Lover of our soul is just a few steps away, one simple choice on our part, but we miss him and his offer of blessing.

As I say the phrase "one simple choice," I know that in fact there is nothing simple about it. Often, it is not a lack of trust in God's *boulema* or *thelema* that keeps us in bed, but rather the murkiness of not knowing the immediate result of putting our feet on the floor. We face a no man's land between making a decision and seeing the final result, where we are left to wonder if we really did the right thing for the right reason at the right time. Did I really need to sacrifice my wants and desires? Did I put myself and my family in harm's way for no good reason? Am I doing this strange thing as a novelty, just to break out of the routine of my life? If I have decided in error, will it take years to undo the effects of this choice? If this is the place you find yourself, I have two words of encouragement for you. First, you are not alone in these fears, and if you are willing to be honest about your doubts, you will find both inspiration and comfort from the stories of others, including those in this book. Second, God's *boulema* will be accomplished. Good decision or bad decision, good timing or bad timing, he will not be denied. He is not only one who redeems, he is our Redeemer. If there is anything we learn from all of the decisions recorded in the Bible, noble and scandalous and everything in between, it is that God can use anything for his glory, including our flawed moral will.

One of the most astounding things to me about God is that, despite our poor choices and our rudeness toward him, he just keeps coming back with more offers of blessing. Why? Because he *chooses* to. God chooses to love the unlovely. He chooses to shepherd the blind and the lame. He chooses to bless those who would curse him. This is perhaps the starkest example of the all-out conflict between the way of the Spirit and our way of doing things. As Paul says in Rom 8:7–8, "The mind governed by the flesh is hostile to God; it does not submit to God's law, nor can it do so. Those who are in the realm of the flesh cannot please God." God wants to bless us, and he will pursue us to accomplish that *thelema*, but at some point, we have to get out of bed and answer the door. A verse that is often quoted from Revelation as a salvation verse was originally intended for a Christian audience: "Here I am! I stand at the door and knock. If anyone hears my voice and opens the door, I will come in and eat with that person, and they with me" (Rev 3:20). This sounds very similar to the situation presented poetically in Song of Songs 5: God does not change; he continually offers the opportunity for blessing. The question for us, every day, is whether we will "choose life."

The chapters in the remainder of this book put some meat on the skeletal frame outlined here. The characters who are the focus of each chapter have been deliberately chosen to illustrate the complementary nature of and the tension that exists between God's choices and our own. One decision enhances the other, yet the road to that agreement can sometimes be a rocky one: the choice for mission we see in the life of Abraham, the choice for identity so pivotal in the life of Jacob, the choice for obedience found throughout the life of Joseph, the choice for righteousness that exemplified Job's life, the choice for worship that was the hallmark of David's life, the choice for anointing Elisha pursued in his life, the choice for suffering that characterized Paul's life, and the choice for redemption found throughout the story of Jesus' Advent. In these stories, individuals were called on to make difficult choices. However, those choices were facilitated by the fact that God had already made his choice, and his blessing was on their lives. What choice is God asking you to make in your life? How should you respond? The chapters that follow are intended as a journey of discovery, to see how others have answered those questions before us. I hope you will see that our lives are not so very different from theirs.

Chapter 2

The Choice for Mission: The Life of Abraham

Do you have any spiritual heroes, those who inspire you to greatness with their lives and words? Sometimes our heroes come from the past, those who have already lived yet have left an indelible mark on the world for Christ. But some are surprises to us, giants who we encounter in unexpected ways while they are still living: Those who are not just inspirations, but also a kind of spiritual father or mother, birthing something in us that wasn't there before. One of those people for me was John Stott, the grand old British theologian and missiologist, now passed away. When I first encountered him, I was barely aware of him being a principal author of *The Lausanne Covenant*, and I had no idea he was chaplain to the Queen of England or that the initials C.B.E. came after his name. For me, he was just a plenary speaker at the 1976 Urbana missions conference. Yet, by the end of that conference, I had not only heard his powerful words, but actually spoken with the man and, most crucially, been inspired toward a life of mission.

What I heard at that conference was Stott's sweeping missional narrative, "The Living God is a Missionary God," captured later as a chapter in the book *Perspectives on the World Christian Movement*. There were so many new ideas for me in that talk, but perhaps the most profound revelation was that mission pre-dated the New Testament church. We see evidence of God's choice for mission as far back as Genesis 10. There we are given a table of nations that came from Noah's family following the flood. It does not single out the Jewish people, nor any people for that matter. All nations are included, demonstrating that ethnic and cultural diversity are part of God's creative design.

Then, in Gen 11:4 we read that human beings made the bold statement, "... 'Come, let us build ourselves a city, with a tower that reaches to the heavens, so that we may make a name for ourselves ...,'" and in doing so, declared their independence from God. So, God confused them by giving every people group their own language, and this resulted in their dispersion throughout the world. Although judgment is a very negative thing, we must understand that dispersion is one way in which God works his *boulema* in the world: dispersion of the nations at Babel, dispersion of the people of Israel into exile, dispersion of the apostles and other believers after the fall of Jerusalem. In particular, the dispersion at Babel set the stage for God's declaration of promise concerning all future generations, including ours.

It is in this context that we encounter the first four verses of Genesis chapter 12, the true beginning of mission in the Bible:

> The Lord had said to Abram, "Go from your country, your people and your father's household to the land I will show you.
>
> "I will make you into a great nation,
> and I will bless you;
> I will make your name great,
> and you will be a blessing.
> I will bless those who bless you,
> and whoever curses you I will curse;
> and all peoples on earth
> will be blessed through you."
>
> So Abram left, as the Lord had told him, and Lot went with him. Abram was seventy-five years old when he set out from Haran.

This is the proclamation of God's *boulema* to bless the nations. As Stott says, "These are perhaps the most unifying verses in the Bible; the whole of God's purpose is encapsulated here."[1] It was (and is) his intention to bless all the families of the earth through Abram and his spiritual descendants. But still, Abram (soon to be Abraham) had to choose whether or not to take God up on his offer of blessing, to leave his home and become the first missionary. It's important to remember that before Abram was chosen for mission, his father Terah had made the first move toward the land of Canaan, what would later be known as the Promised Land. Gen 11:31 says, "Terah took his son Abram, his grandson Lot son of Haran, and his daughter-in-law Sarai, the wife of his son Abram, and together they set out from Ur of the Chaldeans to go to Canaan. But when they came to Harran, they settled there." And this is where Abram heard from God about his mission. Why had Terah stopped? We aren't told, but we are informed in the last verse of Genesis 11 that Abram and his family remained in Harran until Terah died. That's a long time for Abram to get comfortable where he was, in his relationships, his work, his priorities.

The world's emphasis is on getting out of the situation we're in—a bad relationship, a bad job—rather than having a calling *to* something else. The Israelites were led out of Egypt, but they were also led to the Promised Land. Likewise with Abram and his family. It is natural, when called to leave the familiar (not even geographically, but perhaps emotionally) to focus on what is being given up, rather than on what God has in store for us. But we have to be convinced that it is God who knows the beginning from the end, not us. It is God who knows the plans he has for our lives, not us. It is a sign of maturity in our relationship with God when we can ask the question, "what's next?" without fear, but instead with assurance and even excitement. In fact, probably even better than asking the question "what's next?" is to simply say to God, "show your glory," to have our moral will agree with his *boulema*. That's a choice we make. Transitions in our lives then become less about us and our feelings of helplessness and more about anticipating how God's *boulema* will unfold and how his *thelema* will demonstrate his love and care for us and the world.

1. Stott, "The Living God is a Missionary God," 3

As Stott points out, the promise of God to Abram is actually three promises in one. It was first of all a promise of heritage. God intends to make from Abram a "great nation." The name Abram means "exalted father." Although this is an honorable name, God had something even more significant in mind. He would change Abram's name to Abraham, a forward-looking name meaning "father of a multitude." How big is a multitude? Abram wouldn't have understood it if God merely told him—God had to show him the stars in the sky to help him grasp the idea. We see the ultimate fulfillment of this promise in John's vision of Rev 7:9: "After this I looked, and there before me was a great multitude that no one could count, from every nation, tribe, people and language, standing before the throne and before the Lamb. They were wearing white robes and were holding palm branches in their hands."

Who makes up this multitude? It's us—you and me—standing alongside people from every nation, tribe, and people group. I believe God's promise of family has never been more significant than it is today, a time in which families are disintegrating and people, especially young people, are feeling more isolated than ever. Stunningly, according to Revelation, those who we never knew in this life will be our family for all eternity.

Secondly, it was a promise of land. Abram was to leave his homeland, and in return, God would show him another country. Everyone with a missional calling has been required to exchange his or her present life and goals for God's promises. Abram graciously allowed his nephew Lot to choose where he wanted to settle, and Lot chose the fertile Jordan valley. This, then, defined the land that God would give Abram; essentially, it was everything else. But it wasn't just physical land that was being promised. A couple thousand years later, the writer of Hebrews declared that we have access to a spiritual Promised Land as well: "Therefore, since the promise of entering his rest still stands, let us be careful that none of you be found to have fallen short of it. For we also have had the good news proclaimed to us, just as they did; but the message they heard was of no value to them, because they did not share the faith of those who obeyed. Now we who have believed enter that rest . . . " (Heb 4:1–3). The "they" being referred to is Moses and the Israelites, who could not enter the "rest" of the Promised Land, yet spiritually such a rest is open to us now through faith in Jesus Christ. In this busy world of ours where we move frantically from one activity to the next is there anything our spirits crave more than rest? Not simply inactivity, but deep, peaceful abiding in God's presence. This is not something only to be anticipated, but we are told we can "enter that rest" right now through faith in Jesus.

Third, it was a promise of blessing. The words "bless," "blessing," or "blessed" are mentioned five times in Gen 12:2–3. From the beginning, this blessing was intended for all humankind. At its heart is the covenant that God makes between himself and Abram. Ultimately, this blessing is the gift of faith and the justification that comes by faith. Paul makes this connection in Rom 4:22–25: "This is why 'it was credited to him as righteousness.' The words 'it was credited to him' were written not for him alone, but also for us, to whom God will credit righteousness—for us who believe in him who raised Jesus our Lord from the dead. He was delivered over to death for our sins and was raised to life for our justification." Once God changed Abram's name to Abraham, he identified himself with Abraham and his descendants, saying, "I will be their God" (Gen 17:8). This is the greatest blessing that any of us can ever receive. Christ bore our curse that we might inherit Abraham's blessing, the blessing of justification and the indwelling Holy Spirit. This is the reason we have eternity and our new family to look forward to, and it is the reason we can rest now. God has us, and he won't let go.

What do these promises have to do with mission and missional calling? There are two parts to every calling: God's choice and our choice. God chose Abram, and Abram chose to go. God also chose to fulfill each of the promises, the rewards for obedience. He reveals himself as a missional God because he blessed not just Abraham, not just his descendants, but all the nations of the world. God was not just choosing a people to bless, but rather a people *through* whom he could bless the entire human race. From the beginning, God intended to bring his Kingdom to earth, and he designed mission to be the vehicle for that blessing. The psalmist understood this. Ps 67:1–2 proclaims:

> May God be gracious to us and bless us
>   and make his face shine on us—
> so that your ways may be known on earth,
>   your salvation among all nations.

God says in Exod 19:6 that the nation of Israel was designed to be "a kingdom of priests and a holy nation," and that priestly role was to represent God among the nations. Now, even as I relay the words " . . . a kingdom of priests and a holy nation . . . ," you may actually be thinking of a different verse, 1 Pet 2:9, which states, "But you are a chosen people, a royal priesthood, a holy nation, God's special possession, that you may declare the praises of him who called you out of darkness into his wonderful light." To whom is Peter referring? Well, if you are a believer in Jesus Christ, he is referring to *you*. Here is the revelation for us today: The promise given to Abraham by God lives on today, in us. Paul puts it this way in Gal 3:17–18, 22, 26–29:

> What I mean is this: The law, introduced 430 years later, does not set aside the covenant previously established by God and thus do away with the promise. For if the inheritance depends on the law, then it no longer depends on the promise; but God in his grace gave it to Abraham through a promise . . . But Scripture has locked up everything under the control of sin, so that what was promised, being given through faith in Jesus Christ, might be given to those who believe . . . So in Christ Jesus you are all children of God through faith, for all of you who were baptized into Christ have clothed yourselves with Christ. There is neither Jew nor Gentile, neither slave nor free, nor is there male and female, for you are all one in Christ Jesus. If you belong to Christ, then you are Abraham's seed, and heirs according to the promise.

These words must have been staggering to Paul's readers, especially the Jews who had endeavored to keep the Law all their lives. Essentially, Paul is saying that because Jesus fulfilled the requirements of the Law through his death and resurrection, we don't have to talk about the Law anymore. Paul skips over the 1500 year history of the Law and makes a direct connection between believers in Christ and Abraham and his promise. Paul's not-so-subtle message is that we now have a vested interest in seeing the promise fulfilled in the world.

Therefore, it is crucial to grasp the point that these promises do not merely apply to the great by and by. Certainly, we have the hope of eternity and our family in heaven to look forward to, but the promises just mentioned are intended to be prime movers for our lives here on earth, right now. It's easy to say, "one day I might be a missionary," but it's much more accurate to say, "I *am* a missionary." We are all on mission; it is part and parcel of being a Christian. There's a saying that refers to the story of Jesus inviting Peter to walk on the water with him: It's crowded in the boat, but there's plenty of room on the water. After all, what is the purpose of faith if we aren't stepping out of the boat? Why all these promises if not to allow us to hold tight to God's hand in unfamiliar and even threatening circumstances? This is not "I'll fly away" theology. This is the "already but not yet" of the Kingdom of heaven.

One final point: these promises are not just for us—those who are chosen by God—but they are intended for everyone. Jesus makes the connection between the preaching of the Gospel to the nations and his eventual return when he says in Matt 24:14, "And this gospel of the kingdom will be preached in the whole world as a testimony to all nations, and then the end will come." Today, we need to come to a new understanding of our God as the God of "all peoples on earth." There are no off-limits areas to God, only to our natural way of thinking. There are no walls with God, only with our human way of doing things. No individual, people, or nation exists beyond God's love, even though our upbringing might lead us to believe otherwise. The God of Abraham is the God of us all, and he intends to bring the blessing of Abraham to all peoples through us, his followers.

As we read earlier, we are a chosen people, or said another way, God has already made his choice. As J.R. Woodward states, "God's mission is to redeem the world and restore it to its intended purpose. The church exists to fulfill God's mission, and when we participate in God's mission we become living signs of God's intended future for the world, bringing glory to God. In other words, mission exists because God is a missionary God."[2] It is inescapable: Every believer possesses a missional calling. The question is whether we will align our moral will with our Father's *boulema* and *thelema*, as Abraham did, agreeing to be blessed and to be a blessing.

2. Woodward, *Creating a Missional Culture*, 28.

Chapter 3

The Choice for Identity: The Life of Jacob

Is there any starker example of the choices God makes than the life of Jacob? At the beginning of the Book of Malachi, God is speaking to the nation of Israel and he says:

> "I have loved you," says the Lord.
>
> "But you ask, 'How have you loved us?'
>
> "Was not Esau Jacob's brother?" declares the Lord. "Yet I have loved Jacob, but Esau I have hated, and I have turned his hill country into a wasteland and left his inheritance to the desert jackals." (Mal 1:2–3)

These words are quoted by the Apostle Paul under the New Covenant in Rom 9:13. As I mentioned in the first chapter, we like to dwell on the winners of the Bible without fully considering the fact that often, in the process of one person winning, inevitably someone else loses. Yet we see in this the silver lining of God's grace, as Paul continues in Rom 9:22–23: "What if God, although choosing to show his wrath and make his power known, bore with great patience the objects of his wrath—prepared for destruction? What if he did this to make the riches of his glory known to the objects of his mercy, whom he prepared in advance for glory . . . ?"

As we will see, there is a redemptive aspect of Jacob's story for both Jacob and Esau, but it was a long road for both of them, and for Jacob it required a complete transformation of his identity. Jacob was so named by his parents, but toward the end of his life he was known by the name Israel, the name God gave him. This name change, and what it has to do with choices, is the focus of this chapter.

Do you like your name? Have you ever wanted to change your name? I like the name Paul because I was named for the Apostle Paul, but I don't like that it means "small." Until about a week before our son was born, my wife and I were going to name him Michael, but at the last minute we changed it to Carl, more for the way it sounds than what it means (Carl never cared for the fact that his name means "farmer"). Though many times parents will choose a name for a child without knowing what it means, God seems to put a premium on names and their meanings, and it is a major event in the Bible when someone's name is changed.

It is worthwhile to consider the lives of those people in the Bible who had their names changed by God. The before and after picture of their lives and the change that took place is often very vivid: Abram who became Abraham, Sarai who became Sarah, Jacob who became Israel, Simon who became Peter, Saul who became Paul. One of the greatest promises given in the Book of Revelation is, as a reward for overcoming evil, Jesus would give the church a new name or write a new name on them. Names are so important to God that at times he steps in and gives the name of a new baby to the parents even before the baby's birth—names such as John for John the Baptist, and Jesus.

Still, we can hardly help the name we are given at birth. Gen 25:24–26 tells us: "When the time came for her to give birth, there were twin boys in her womb. The first to come out was red, and his whole body was like a hairy garment; so they named him Esau. After this, his brother came out, with his hand grasping Esau's heel; so he was named Jacob. Isaac was sixty years old when Rebekah gave birth to them." The name Jacob literally means "one who grasps the heel," which is a reference to him having hold of the heel of his twin brother Esau when the two of them were born. But the name also has a figurative meaning, referring to somebody who deceives others. Can you imagine having been given a name like this, with all of the baggage associated with it in the Hebrew language? As Chimamanda Adichie has poignantly observed, *"Show a people as one thing, only one thing, over and over again, and that is what they become."*[1] It shouldn't have been a surprise to anyone, then, that Jacob's life was dominated by deception and grasping for what belonged to others.

But we need to understand the name "deceiver" as more than just a label or representing more than some character flaw. What it actually represented was, I believe, a generations-old curse, which was finally broken by God when he gave Jacob his new name of Israel. Understood in this way, Jacob and Israel become more than just names, and Jacob's wrestling match with the angel becomes more than just an oddity of Scripture (Gen 32).

When Jacob met the angel, he was returning to Bethel, which is a key location in the Promised Land. Bethel means House of God, and the name was given by Jacob because God appeared to him there and promised to bless his descendants in that land. This was God's *boulema*, which had also been proclaimed over Jacob's progenitors. It was at Bethel that Abram, Jacob's grandfather, first pitched his tent in the Promised Land. It was also at Bethel that Abram made the decision to go with Sarai to Egypt because of the famine in Canaan (Gen 12:8), and therefore, it was at Bethel that deception was first conceived in Abram's mind, to lie to the king of Egypt and say that Sarai was Abram's sister, not his wife. We read about this in Gen 12:10–13: "Now there was a famine in the land, and Abram went down to Egypt to live there for a while because the famine was severe. As he was about to enter Egypt, he said to his wife Sarai, 'I know what a beautiful woman you are. When the Egyptians see you, they will say, "This is his wife." Then they will kill me but will let you live. Say you are my sister, so that I will be treated well for your sake and my life will be spared because of you.'"

Deception of any kind is generally conceived out of a desire for self-protection. Abram was trying to keep from being killed; however, most of us are simply trying to keep ourselves from being embarrassed or humiliated. So we just change a few facts—add one

1. Adichie, *The Danger of a Single Story*, video

in, leave one out. A white lie, we might call it. It's designed to make us look better, or at least different, from reality. And everything went well for Abram until God blew the whistle on him by sending diseases into Pharaoh's house, where Sarai had been taken, and the king kicked Abram and his family out of the country (note especially that this is the first of two times Abram lied about his wife).

Seen in isolation, this story may appear insignificant. But when viewed in light of God's words about the sins of the fathers being visited on following generations (Num 14:18), we understand that Abram's deception opened a door to heartache and disappointment in his family for generations to come. We can't help but notice that Isaac, Abram's son, repeated the sin of his father a generation later (Gen 26:1,7). And then came Jacob, the master deceiver.

Apparently, Isaac and Rebekah each had their favorite among the twins: Isaac chose Esau, and Rebekah chose Jacob. Thus, there was not merely sibling rivalry between Jacob and Esau, but literally the whole house was divided, and they were divided primarily over the issue of birthright and blessing. As a result, this became an obsession for Jacob, and he began looking for any means by which he might obtain these things from Esau.

Deception is always looking for an opportunity, an open door. Jacob found the open door to Esau's birthright through Esau's physical hunger (Gen 25), and the chance at Esau's blessing came through Isaac's physical blindness, with Rebekah's assistance (Gen 27). But both of these physical doors had spiritual parallels: Esau's hunger caused him to despise his birthright (Gen 25:34), and Isaac's physical blindness caused him to be spiritually short-sighted, forgetting (or choosing not to remember) that God had said the older would serve the younger (Gen 25:23). Essentially, everyone was doing what was right in his own eyes, another fruit of deception. Rebekah became a manipulative enabler (Gen 27:41–28:2), Esau went into full rebellion (Gen 28:6–9), and Jacob would himself become a victim of deception at the hands of his father-in-law Laban, when he was forced to marry a woman he did not love (Gen 29). Fruits of the deception tree include mistrust and division, and by now these fruits were fully ripened. The family of promise was being ripped apart and was in great danger of collapse.

Eventually, Jacob ran from Laban, even as he was already running from Esau. When it looked like Esau would catch up with and kill Jacob, he finally turned to God and repented, calling himself " . . . unworthy of all the kindness and faithfulness . . . " God had shown him, and asking God to save him (Gen 32:10–11).

I believe that what Jacob accomplished with this act of repentance is similar to the words spoken by the prophet in Isa 52:2 many centuries after Jacob died:

> Shake off your dust;
> rise up, sit enthroned, Jerusalem.
> Free yourself from the chains on your neck,
> Daughter Zion, now a captive.

In the case of Jacob, the chains he wore were the curse of deception that ran through his family, and on the way to Bethel, he finally understood that he didn't have to live with those chains any longer. The wrestling match with the angel is still a bit of a mystery, but I think it has something to do with Jacob finally taking responsibility for the condition of his life and his family. That is why Jacob says to the angel that he will not let him go until he is blessed. It was not Jacob grasping for someone else's blessing, like before; he was choosing God's *thelema* for *him*. For Jacob it was a matter of life and death. Somehow he knew that with the blessing there would also be deliverance, both physical and spiritual, but without it the curse would continue to plague his children and their children as it had plagued him.

The immediate outcome of the struggle between Jacob and the angel was a blessing and a new name, Israel, which literally means "he who wrestles with God." But as we study the life of Israel after the wrestling match, we see the fruit that came from breaking the curse: he got rid of all idols and foreign gods in his household (Gen 35), he reconciled and stood side-by-side with Esau when they buried their father Isaac (Gen 35), and ultimately he blessed each of his children with unique and God-inspired blessings before his death (Gen 49). His "grasping" days were over, and as a result the nation of Israel was blessed. Jacob had chosen to break away from the label that had been placed on him at birth and chose instead the identity God had for him. The blessing of Israel's children and grandchildren recounted for us in Gen 48:15–16 is especially sweet when we think about his name change:

> Then he blessed Joseph and said,
> "May the God before whom my fathers
> Abraham and Isaac walked faithfully,
> the God who has been my shepherd
> all my life to this day,
> the Angel who has delivered me from all harm
> —may he bless these boys.
> May they be called by my name
> and the names of my fathers Abraham and Isaac,
> and may they increase greatly
> on the earth."

I asked you earlier if you would change your name if you had the chance. But really, we have many names, not just the name given to us by our parents. There is a song that says:

> *I will change your name*
> *You shall no longer be called*
> *Wounded, outcast*
> *Lonely or afraid*[2]

I would say this is an apt description of Jacob when the angel found him. But, it is also appropriate for many of us today—these are just some of the names that we acquire as we live our lives. The names are obviously not from God. Perhaps some of them are due to decisions we ourselves have made, but some of them are also due to generational curses, as with Jacob. Either way, when we

2. Butler, *I Will Change Your Name*, song

choose to accept and live with a name, it comes to define us. No matter how long we've been bound by the chains, however, God desires to change these names. The song continues:

> *I will change your name*
> *Your new name shall be*
> *Confidence, joyfulness*
> *Overcoming one*
> *Faithfulness, friend of God*
> *One who seeks my face*[3]

One time I was asking God in prayer how I could read the Gospels in a new way, to gain some kind of fresh understanding from these books I had read all my life. I was reminded of when Jesus said to his disciples that he no longer called them servants but rather friends. I felt like God was saying to me, "Jesus already knows everything about you as *his* friend. Read the Gospels to find out more about *your* friend Jesus." It's amazing what you can learn from the Gospels when you ask the question, "What is my friend Jesus trying to tell me about himself?" In this way, I felt like God was changing my name from spiritually "lonely" to "friend of God." God is our Redeemer—he loves to bring about change in our lives, if we choose to let him. What name of yours would you like God to change? Don't let go of him until he blesses you.

3. Ibid.

Chapter 4

The Choice for Obedience: The Life of Joseph

I LOVE BASEBALL. I would go to games all the time if I could afford it. And for good or for bad, I have passed on this addiction to my son, with whom I have seen countless games. One year, quite unexpectedly, a minor league team started up in our little town. This was the answer to an unutterable prayer: games with cheap tickets played right at our door. In the early days of the team, we had a lot of "personal space" at the games: We were the few, the proud. One evening we were sitting in the stands with no one else close by, both of us wearing our gloves in the hope of catching a foul ball (don't judge me). Suddenly, it happened! The batter swung and hit a towering foul ball back toward the stands. My son and I were immediately on guard, thinking we would have to make some kind of dramatic dive to catch the ball. But as we followed the path of the ball in the air, surprisingly, it seemed to be coming directly toward us. We were ready to move, but it was like the ball was saying, "Just wait there." So, we stuck out our gloves, and as it turned out, mine was literally sitting on top of my son's so that when the ball landed in my glove, we were like a baseball layer cake: glove, glove, ball. It's hard to describe the feeling for a die-hard baseball fan. It was like we had been chosen, singled out for favor and blessing. Has that happened to you before, when you felt like heaven and earth were moved just so you could be blessed? This is how I think about Joseph, Jacob's favorite.

Joseph is one of the classic "deep selects" from the biblical account—so many brothers ahead of him in the pecking order, such an unlikely candidate to receive favor from the God of the universe. But as with all of the biblical characters we're looking at, Joseph's strength was his agreement with God's plan, as unlikely as it seemed. In fact, it was this initial agreement that got him in trouble with his family. Gen 37:5–11 recounts:

> Joseph had a dream, and when he told it to his brothers, they hated him all the more. He said to them, "Listen to this dream I had: We were binding sheaves of grain out in the field when suddenly my sheaf rose and stood upright, while your sheaves gathered around mine and bowed down to it." His brothers said to him, "Do you intend to reign over us? Will you actually rule us?" And they hated him all the more because of his dream and what he had said. Then he had another dream, and he told it to his brothers. "Listen," he said, "I had another dream, and this time the sun and moon and eleven stars were bowing down to me." When he told his father as well as his brothers, his father rebuked him and said, "What is this dream you had? Will your mother and I and your brothers actually come and bow down to the ground before you?" His brothers were jealous of him, but his father kept the matter in mind.

Many have said that Joseph was full of pride when he told his family about the dreams he had of them worshipping him, but I don't believe pride was the issue. I don't believe pride was ever an issue with Joseph. In fact, Joseph is one of my biblical heroes precisely because his obedience was so pure and so enduring. I believe that when Joseph retold his dreams, he was simply agreeing with what God had shown him, that powerful agreement of human moral will with God's *boulema* and *thelema*. However, almost certainly Joseph did not understand the full implication of his agreement.

One of the greatest tests of obedience we see in Scripture is the faithful retelling of God's revelation by his prophets because it usually meant trouble for the teller. This was an early test for

Joseph, who in adulthood would be called on to relay hard words to people. From the beginning there was a fidelity to Joseph's faith, a commitment to truth, a fundamental agreement with God's *boulema*. His father Jacob, who as a younger man had a dream about a ladder extending to heaven with angels ascending and descending on it, felt obligated culturally to rebuke Joseph after hearing about his dreams, but spiritually held onto the mystery as a potential clue to his son's own chosen-ness. For Joseph's part, it is unlikely that he understood everything the dream meant, but he knew it was from God, and that it was intended for him.

Before I ever came to Ukraine as a missionary, God had to prepare me—calling me, cleaning me out, and filling me up with his presence. During that time of preparation, he gave me a very special verse, which was just for me. It is Isa 55:5:

> "Surely you will summon nations you know not,
>   and nations you do not know will come running to you,
> because of the LORD your God,
>   the Holy One of Israel,
>   for he has endowed you with splendor."

I received this verse as God's promise to me, but because it came before the invitation to Ukraine, I had no idea of the significance of it for my life. Only a year later, I was in Ukraine preaching to a room full of people from the different countries of the former Soviet Union. In that moment, the Isaiah verse flashed across my mind, and I realized I was seeing the fulfillment of God's promise to me. This kind of vision is something that can keep us going even in the darkest hour of trial and temptation.

One reason Joseph could choose to obey and remain faithful in his obedience was the depth of his character. We do not simply choose one day to obey God and suddenly find that we are full of faith, perseverance, and hope. It is true that character is borne out of suffering, as Paul says in Romans 5, but it is also true that there must exist a rich topsoil of character for obedience to take root. Though the basis for God's choices are not always obvious, I would venture to say that most of the time it has to do with character and the capacity for obedience. How do we know that Joseph was a man of integrity, even prior to his trials? One clue is that the sharing of the dreams God had given him with his entire family took place when he was only seventeen years old.

The narrative of Joseph's life contained in the Book of Genesis takes up many chapters, but let's focus on three principles of obedience that resulted from godly character as we find them in Genesis chapter 39.

Principle 1 Joseph stood firm, whether the test was as a result of prosperity or adversity. Gen 39:1–10 tells us:

> Now Joseph had been taken down to Egypt. Potiphar, an Egyptian who was one of Pharaoh's officials, the captain of the guard, bought him from the Ishmaelites who had taken him there. The LORD was with Joseph so that he prospered, and he lived in the house of his Egyptian master. When his master saw that the LORD was with him and that the LORD gave him success in everything he did, Joseph found favor in his eyes and became his attendant. Potiphar put him in charge of his household, and he entrusted to his care everything he owned. From the time he put him in charge of his household and of all that he owned, the LORD blessed the household of the Egyptian because of Joseph. The blessing of the LORD was on everything Potiphar had, both in the house and in the field. So Potiphar left everything he had in Joseph's care; with Joseph in charge, he did not concern himself with anything except the food he ate. Now Joseph was well-built and handsome, and after a while his master's wife took notice of Joseph and said, "Come to bed with me!" But he refused. "With me in charge," he told her, "my master does not concern himself with anything in the house; everything he owns he has entrusted to my care. No one is greater in this house than I am. My master has withheld nothing from me except you, because you are his wife. How then could I do such a wicked thing and sin against God?" And though she spoke to Joseph day after day, he refused to go to bed with her or even be with her.

The Apostle Paul frames Joseph's perspective this way in Phil 4:11–13, " . . . I have learned to be content whatever the circumstances. I know what it is to be in need, and I know what it is to have plenty. I have learned the secret of being content in any and every situation, whether well fed or hungry, whether living in plenty or in want. I can do all this through him who gives me strength." Despite Joseph growing up as Jacob's favorite son, wearing the multi-colored coat that announced to everyone his favored status, Joseph never took advantage of that position. And, that pattern of living continued in Egypt. Joseph was apparently not swayed by possessions or people's esteem of him. Further, he knew the limit of his authority, and he determined not to overstep that authority. We often take our chosen-ness too far; we presume on God and his beneficence. For many, it is like winning the lottery. We have nothing of our own, we become rich, and then we spend our wealth until it is gone. Joseph, on the other hand, when he was blessed, took great care to cultivate that blessing. He measured out the faithfulness and obedience needed for the situation, being ever-mindful of the limit of his anointing. Gal 6:3–5 says, "If anyone thinks they are something when they are not, they deceive themselves. Each one should test their own actions. Then they can take pride in themselves alone, without comparing themselves to someone else, for each one should carry their own load." This way of living is rare in our day, even among Christians, and I believe it needs to be recaptured by people of faith.

Principle 2 Joseph did what was right even when no one was looking. The story continues in Gen 39:11–18:

> One day he went into the house to attend to his duties, and none of the household servants was inside. She caught him by his cloak and said, "Come to bed with me!" But he left his cloak in her hand and ran out of the house. When she saw that he had left his cloak in her hand and had run out of the house, she called her household servants. "Look," she said to them, "this Hebrew has been brought to us to make sport of us! He came in here to sleep with me, but I screamed. When he heard me scream for help, he left his cloak beside me and ran

> out of the house." She kept his cloak beside her until his master came home. Then she told him this story: "That Hebrew slave you brought us came to me to make sport of me. But as soon as I screamed for help, he left his cloak beside me and ran out of the house."

Jesus had a lot to say about this particular aspect of obedience. It is not obedience for obedience's sake, or obedience for my own sake, but obedience for God's sake. Jesus' primary counter-example of this principle was the Pharisees: "And when you pray, do not be like the hypocrites, for they love to pray standing in the synagogues and on the street corners to be seen by others. Truly I tell you, they have received their reward in full. But when you pray, go into your room, close the door and pray to your Father, who is unseen. Then your Father, who sees what is done in secret, will reward you" (Matt 6:5–6). Joseph understood that the reward standing in front of him, Potiphar's wife, could hardly compare with the reward of authority and respect he commanded under Potiphar. Yet, this was not the end of the comparisons. Joseph also had his dreams in his back pocket, something God had placed in him at a young age to help him weather exactly these kinds of storms. His calling was "out there" in the future, and nothing would deter him from seeing its fulfillment. He had chosen a level of obedience that few believers do: the understanding and the lived-reality that the right thing, done in secret, is seen and rewarded by the One who matters most. We might say that at this point his obedience was almost "mindless." Not that it was automatic, but rather that his soul (mind, will, and emotions) was not the obstacle it so often is for us. This kind of obedience is only possible when we are Spirit-led, and in particular, when our own spirit, which agrees with the Holy Spirit (Rom 8:16), takes the lead in our life. Of course, it is completely counter-cultural to deny ourselves anything in this modern age of ours. We are constantly encouraged to feed our bodies, our minds, our emotions. But do we feed our spirits? If we do not, we shouldn't be surprised that our capacity for obedience, especially when no one is looking, is different from that of Joseph's.

Principle 3 Joseph's character was best displayed through times of crisis. Joseph's trifecta of tribulation concludes with Gen 39:19–23:

> When his master heard the story his wife told him, saying, "This is how your slave treated me," he burned with anger. Joseph's master took him and put him in prison, the place where the king's prisoners were confined. But while Joseph was there in the prison, the LORD was with him; he showed him kindness and granted him favor in the eyes of the prison warden. So the warden put Joseph in charge of all those held in the prison, and he was made responsible for all that was done there. The warden paid no attention to anything under Joseph's care, because the LORD was with Joseph and gave him success in whatever he did.

It's hard to keep a good person down, yet it's hard to be that good person. It's easy when you know the end of the story, but difficult when you're in the midst of it. Joseph was convinced that his own lack of understanding of what was happening said absolutely nothing about God's care or concern for him. He understood that the crisis wasn't the most important thing, as we often think, but rather his response to the crisis. Call it a test, call it whatever you want. Our lives are full of these moments when we have a choice for or against obedience, for or against God's *boulema*. Is our main goal to relieve the suffering or to find where the suffering is leading? Do we have sufficient character to fall back on in difficult circumstances or does our character collapse like a two-legged stool?

Joseph endured a remarkable series of negative circumstances in his life that was completely out of his control: being thrown into a pit and left for dead by his brothers, being sold into slavery and sent to another country, being wrongly imprisoned in that country, being forgotten in prison for two years by a man Joseph had helped. But somehow God used these horrible circumstances to save an entire region of the world from starvation. As Joseph said to his brothers at the end of the story, "You intended to harm me, but God intended it for good to accomplish what is now being done, the saving of many lives" (Gen 50:20).

The greatest disappointments can be transformed by God into blessing because that is his *thelema* for us. Still, we have our part to play. Joseph never complained, and he never blamed God for his circumstances; he simply believed that his dream would come true. And he maintained this belief through his time in slavery and through two years of being wrongly imprisoned. I love the title of a Eugene Peterson book, taken from a Nietzsche quote: *A Long Obedience in the Same Direction*. I believe it is this kind of perseverance in trial that brings maximum glory to God. It's the very reason he chooses us in the first place.

Chapter 5

The Choice for Righteousness: The Life of Job

The Book of Job contains this interesting little vignette in chapter 1:

> One day the angels came to present themselves before the Lord, and Satan also came with them. The Lord said to Satan, "Where have you come from?" Satan answered the Lord, "From roaming throughout the earth, going back and forth on it." Then the Lord said to Satan, "Have you considered my servant Job? There is no one on earth like him; he is blameless and upright, a man who fears God and shuns evil." "Does Job fear God for nothing?" Satan replied. "Have you not put a hedge around him and his household and everything he has? You have blessed the work of his hands, so that his flocks and herds are spread throughout the land. But now stretch out your hand and strike everything he has, and he will surely curse you to your face." The Lord said to Satan, "Very well, then, everything he has is in your power, but on the man himself do not lay a finger." Then Satan went out from the presence of the Lord. (vss 6–12)

What about this pesky opening scene from the Book of Job? What are we supposed to make of this peek behind the curtain, so to speak, of this conversation between God and Satan? Job was not privileged to know about this conversation before his trials, nor did God inform him at the end of the story. It is only for the reader's eyes. What are we supposed to think about the fact that

God actually draws Satan's attention to Job, almost saying, "Make sure you don't miss this one!"

Surely, God knows that Satan will bring everything to bear in attacking Job, without mercy. Yet not once, but twice in the course of two chapters, God makes it a point to elevate Job so that Satan can't possibly miss him. If we only see Job as the suffering saint, then we might be tempted to feel sorry for him. We might even imagine Job as a defenseless pawn on the chessboard of the universe—not a high-value piece, but something that is sacrificed in the course of playing for the real prize.

And that raises an even more personal question: What about me? What about you? Could the same thing happen to us? What if God points *us* out to Satan? The little drama in chapters 1 and 2 has also been called The Wager by Philip Yancey.[1] It's as if God is saying to Satan, "I bet you can't bring Job down, no matter how hard you try." If we are to believe this is a wager, God is betting that Job's righteousness will save him and that God's *boulema* will be advanced as a result, whereas Satan is betting that Job's righteousness will never make it past the loss of his possessions, his family, and his health.

But none of these scenarios makes much sense to me. First, I can't really imagine *my* heavenly Father regarding any of us as just a pawn; I think he loves us too much to do that. We are not something to be sacrificed in order to win the prize because we *are* the prize. Otherwise, Father God never would have sent his Son Jesus into the world to make the ultimate sacrifice on our behalf. Second, I don't believe the notion of The Wager because I've never known a time in my life when God was not in control or when he played the odds with me. Even when I felt like my life was out of control, God always had a plan, and his plan was always accomplished, sometimes despite me. In the familiar verse from Jer 29:11, God himself says, "'. . . For I know the plans I have for you,' declares the LORD, 'plans to prosper you and not to harm you, plans to give you hope and a future . . .'"

1. Yancey, *Disappointment with God*, 164

No, as Philip Yancey points out, Job was neither poker chip nor pawn. However, there *was* a pawn in the story. There was someone in the story of the Book of Job who understood even less than Job and in the end was ruined as a result of his pride. It was Satan, the one who thought he was in control and understood everything, but who did not understand the verse just mentioned from Jeremiah: God has his *boulema*, he's been carrying out his purpose since before the creation of the world, God will see his plan to completion, and he, not Satan, will be glorified. When God pointed Job out to Satan, he wasn't inviting Satan to take advantage of Job; instead, I believe, he was inviting Satan to be taken advantage of, so that God would receive maximum glory. It has been said that Job was a type of Christ, foreshadowing the suffering and ultimate triumph of Jesus through his death and resurrection. And as it says in 1 John 3:8, "The one who does what is sinful is of the devil, because the devil has been sinning from the beginning. The reason the Son of God appeared was to destroy the devil's work." It's important to understand that because of Jesus' sacrifice, we as believers have the same mission: destroy the work of Satan and bring maximum glory to God.

Of course, we humans are not often afforded a glimpse behind the curtain in our own lives. Many times we have to simply believe that we are part of a cosmic struggle, and our endurance in that struggle makes a difference. My grandmother on my father's side was one of the most righteous people I have known—she delighted in God and in life, she lived simply, and she served sacrificially. She came to live with us after I was born when she was about eighty years old. No one could have known she would live almost thirty more years! Until she was one hundred years old, she cooked and cleaned and vacuumed. She took care of me when my parents went out of town, she taught me to play innumerable card games, and occasionally, she even played whiffle ball with me. All of that changed shortly after she turned one hundred. She took a fall, and that began a slow decline in her health until her death nearly ten years later. During that time, she would lay in bed most of the day, and if you asked her what she needed, she would say "I just want the Lord to take me home."

When a believer passes away prematurely, I have heard people say things like, "They were one of God's favorites, so he took them home early." Well, I can attest to the fact that sometimes God leaves his favorites on earth to suffer, just as he did with Job. Don't get me wrong, I believe suffering has meaning, but many times it's hard to discern that meaning. After the life of service my grandmother had lived, it was difficult to imagine why it was important for her to live in a debilitated condition for so long. We never got to see behind the curtain, to understand something of the cosmic battle being waged, and my grandmother never had everything that was taken from her restored (except in eternity). I do know that my grandmother never lost her faith in a good God, and maybe that was the point. And, she did finally get her wish: At 109 years old, the Lord took her home.

There are many times in my life when I've felt like God's been saying to Satan, "Have you considered my servant Paul?" I've learned a lot of lessons, but one of the most life-changing is fairly simple: We are the army of God, and from time to time, God chooses to send us on dangerous missions, much like Job's. But the key insight from the Book of Job is that God is not picking on us. Instead, it means our heavenly Father is *proud* of us, he *trusts* us, and he *knows* that we have what we need to defeat Satan through our lives. This truth is echoed in 2 Pet 1:3, "His divine power has given us everything we need for a godly life through our knowledge of him who called us by his own glory and goodness." In other words, we were chosen for this mission because he knows that we will be victorious in his strength. That is total affirmation from our heavenly Papa, and I desire it. What about you? Are you ready to live with God's choices? Are you ready for God to choose you, to point you out in a crowd and say to Satan, "Have you considered my servant, (fill in your name)?" Are you ready for God to send you on a mission of cosmic importance, a mission that will bring maximum glory to our Lord while dealing yet another blow to Satan's schemes?

Sometimes, when believers talk about end times or tribulation or the persecuted church in the world, someone will inevitably comment, "I just don't know what I would do in that situation; I don't know if I would be able to remain faithful to God." The truth is that we don't decide to be steadfast in that moment of trial. That choice was made long before: God's choice to save and empower us, and our choice to pursue righteousness. What made Job ready for God to point him out? Simple things, really. He was a generous man who loved his family and the people around him as demonstrated through his care for them physically and spiritually. We hear this throughout the Book of Job. Eliphaz, one of Job's "friends" says of him:

> "Think how you have instructed many,
>   how you have strengthened feeble hands.
> Your words have supported those who stumbled;
>   you have strengthened faltering knees." (Job 4:3–4)

Later, Job fleshes out Eliphaz's account with some details of his life and priorities:

> "Whoever heard me spoke well of me,
>   and those who saw me commended me,
> because I rescued the poor who cried for help,
>   and the fatherless who had none to assist them.
> The one who was dying blessed me;
>   I made the widow's heart sing.
> I put on righteousness as my clothing;
>   justice was my robe and my turban.
> I was eyes to the blind
>   and feet to the lame.
> I was a father to the needy;
>   I took up the case of the stranger.
> I broke the fangs of the wicked
>   and snatched the victims from their teeth."
> (Job 29:11–17)

Job made a powerful choice for righteousness. It is what allowed him to persist despite daunting circumstances. In the middle of his trials, berated by his companions, Job boldly proclaims to them:

> "I will never admit you are in the right;
> till I die, I will not deny my integrity.
> I will maintain my innocence and never let go of it;
> my conscience will not reproach me as long as I live."
> (Job 27:5–6)

Many hundreds of years later, the Apostle Paul would write about the importance of the choice for righteousness in Phil 1:9–11: "And this is my prayer: that your love may abound more and more in knowledge and depth of insight, so that you may be able to discern what is best and may be pure and blameless for the day of Christ, filled with the fruit of righteousness that comes through Jesus Christ—to the glory and praise of God."

Ultimately, God validates Job's choice for righteousness when he has Job pray for his so-called friends at the end of the story. Despite the intervening doubts and angry words Job has spoken about his life, God puts Job in the place of a priest or intercessor. This is yet another way in which Job's experience foreshadows that of Jesus, our "great high priest" (Heb 4:14). Job, like Jesus, lived a righteous life, which eventually resulted in him being exalted before God. The importance of intercession was not an abstraction for Job. At different times, he makes reference to his advocate in heaven, though he never names this intercessor: "Even now my witness is in heaven; my advocate is on high" (Job 16:19), and "I know that my redeemer lives, and that in the end he will stand on the earth" (Job 19:25). Job possesses an insight regarding Christ's intercessory role that predates Jesus' advent on earth by as many as two thousand years, and it is a rock-solid assurance to him in the midst of the worst suffering of his life. In a remarkable turn of events, by the end of Job's story, the suffering one in the greatest need of an intercessor himself becomes an intercessor who is able to influence God's heart.

I don't believe, as Job's companions did, that Job had to go through some sort of exorcism in order to fulfill his calling on earth. Nonetheless, despite his choice for righteousness, it's probably fair to say that before his trials, Job judged his blessings (like all of us do) based on what he could see. We hear this in his words concerning his children at the beginning of the story: " . . . '*Perhaps* my children have sinned and cursed God in their hearts.' . . " (Job 1:5, emphasis added). Job saw God's blessings all around him but feared that what he could *not* see would bring everything to ruin. Isn't that true of all of us? For me personally, I think this is what God's trying to break me of, and it seems to be a process, something like Job's. Fear, at its essence, is a lack of faith, and I have, and have had for much of my Christian life, a profound lack of faith. That was brought into sharp relief when I was a missionary in Ukraine, where so much of the Christian life had to be lived in faith because of a repressive government and the moral depravity stemming from seventy years of Communist rule. The plain truth is, like Job, I need more faith, and apparently like Job, God will stop at nothing to bring about that change in my life. That is his gracious *thelema*. At the beginning of the story, Job acts devotedly, but he does it out of fear of what will happen if he doesn't. In Job 3:25, Job says:

> What I feared has come upon me;
> what I dreaded has happened to me.

But by the end of the story, Job has been forced to face his fears (in his trials, in the whirlwind), and he repents. So, the result of his tribulation was kind of a three for one deal: Satan loses, God wins, and Job is delivered from his fears.

We get to peek behind the curtain in the first two chapters of Job to understand how important Job's suffering was to God. Job never got that chance. But, Job got what he really needed to live his life here on earth, the thing we all need: deliverance from fear. Job went from "seeing is believing" to "believing is seeing," all because of his choice to be righteous and God's choice to be proud of him.

Chapter 6

The Choice for Worship: The Life of David

David was one of God's "deep selects." Because of his birth order and his vocation, he should have lived his life in obscurity and died unknown by the world. But, God had other plans. Ps 78:70–71 says:

> He chose David his servant
> and took him from the sheep pens;
> from tending the sheep he brought him
> to be the shepherd of his people Jacob,
> of Israel his inheritance.

Long before David came on the scene, God was orchestrating his birth and planning his blood line. He chose a foreigner, Ruth, who married into a Jewish family from Bethlehem, lost her husband early, pilgrimaged from her homeland to Bethlehem, met and married the kinsman-redeemer Boaz, and ultimately became David's great grandmother. Clearly, if God chose to bring about the confluence of all those events, he could have easily caused David to be the firstborn among his brothers. But as with all deep selects, God chose to make a point about his sovereignty and about who and what he values. David was a man after God's own heart (Acts 13:22), a musical shepherd boy with the ferocity of a lion, a warrior in the making, an archetype of the King of kings. Psalm 78 concludes with this verse:

And David shepherded them with integrity of heart;
with skillful hands he led them. (Ps 78:72)

Scholars categorize the psalms of David in different ways: by theme, by literary form, by chronology, and so on. There are psalms of thanksgiving, psalms of repentance, psalms of youth, psalms of old age. No matter the kind of psalm, the thread running through all of David's songs is worship. Irrespective of the stage of life or circumstances David found himself in, he was a worshipper first and foremost. First Samuel 16 tells the story of David's initial anointing as king by the prophet Samuel. This took place when David was only about 17 years old. Up to that point, David had been a shepherd tending sheep out in the open field. His early psalms, and his worship of God, reflect his surroundings:

When I consider your heavens,
the work of your fingers,
the moon and the stars,
which you have set in place,
what is mankind that you are mindful of them,
human beings that you care for them?
You have made them a little lower than the angels
and crowned them with glory and honor.
You made them rulers over the works of your hands;
you put everything under their feet:
all flocks and herds,
and the animals of the wild,
the birds in the sky,
and the fish in the sea,
all that swim the paths of the seas.
LORD, our LORD,
how majestic is your name in all the earth! (Ps 8:3–9)

His situation was not unlike that of the shepherds who first heard about the birth of Jesus: "And there were shepherds living out in the fields nearby, keeping watch over their flocks at night" (Luke 2:8). The shepherd's life was simple, yet it required great diligence. There were always predators on the prowl, looking to take advantage of the flock. Those who have been in the military and had to stand watch in the middle of the night know that 99 percent of the time there is absolutely nothing going on. Despite this, because of that other 1 percent, there is no place for inattention. In that situation, your senses are heightened, and you take in more of your surroundings than normal. It follows, then, that David would be overwhelmed with the night sky and what it says about the choices God makes. That consideration led him naturally to worship.

Did you know that we humans were created to praise God? He gives us an insight into his choice through the prophet Isaiah:

> The wild animals honor me,
> the jackals and the owls,
> because I provide water in the wilderness
> and streams in the wasteland,
> to give drink to my people, my chosen,
> the people I formed for myself
> that they may proclaim my praise. (Isa 43:20–21)

Let there be no doubt that when David worshipped thousands of years ago, and when we worship today, it is a direct result of God's choice to place the need to worship in our DNA. We have to worship someone or something. It may be possessions, it may be family and friends, it may be ourselves, it may even be God, but we *will* worship. We just can't help it. David decided early in his life that his worship would be devoted to God, and God honored that decision throughout his life. As another psalmist wrote:

> Blessed are those who have learned to acclaim you,
> who walk in the light of your presence, LORD.
> (Ps 89:15)

However, sometimes that blessing takes a while to work itself out in our lives. It was many years between David's anointing as king and when he actually took the throne. By some estimates, he had to wait upwards of twenty-five years to finally have the crown placed on his head. During this time of waiting Saul, the king on the throne, chased David through the wilderness trying to kill him primarily because he saw him as a threat to his reign. This time of trial was David's preparation and sanctification for being king. Over and over, he threw himself on God's mercies which we hear in the words of the psalms he wrote during this time:

> Save me, O God, by your name;
> vindicate me by your might.
> Hear my prayer, O God;
> listen to the words of my mouth.
> Arrogant foes are attacking me;
> ruthless people are trying to kill me—
> people without regard for God.
> Surely God is my help;
> the Lord is the one who sustains me. (Ps 54:1–4)

As a result of being in extremis on an almost continual basis, David came to the conclusion that the Lord God was his only source of help. This is *exactly* where God wants us and exactly why he allows trials in our lives. God was literally his only hope, and David clung to him for all he was worth.

It was in this time that he made one of the greatest theological statements of his life, Psalm 23. It is a sweeping narrative in which David makes the connection between his boyhood spent tending sheep and his own need for a shepherd. In a flash of Spirit-given inspiration, he realized that what he provided for his sheep is what he needed for his own life: to rest, to be refreshed, to be guided, to be comforted. He looked at the walls of the canyons surrounding him in the wilderness, "the valley of the shadow of death," and he understood that his Shepherd was able to deliver him from fear. And most amazing of all, he was able to look ahead to a time in his life when he would be safe, he would have all of his needs met, and he would be able to do the thing his heart longed to do, to worship for all eternity. So, in the midst of great uncertainty, David chose to worship in his circumstances and thereby gain solace:

> Surely your goodness and love will follow me
>   all the days of my life,
> and I will dwell in the house of the LORD
>   forever. (Ps 23:6)

When David became king, the worship did not stop. In fact, he made certain that 24/7 worship would go on in and around the tabernacle (1 Chr 16). And he didn't stop writing his psalms, but now David writes from a different perspective:

> The king rejoices in your strength, LORD.
>   How great is his joy in the victories you give!
> You have granted him his heart's desire
>   and have not withheld the request of his lips.
> You came to greet him with rich blessings
>   and placed a crown of pure gold on his head.
> He asked you for life, and you gave it to him—
>   length of days, for ever and ever.
> Through the victories you gave, his glory is great;
>   you have bestowed on him splendor and majesty.
> Surely you have granted him unending blessings
>   and made him glad with the joy of your presence.
> For the king trusts in the LORD;
>   through the unfailing love of the Most High
>   he will not be shaken. (Ps 21:1–7)

It is crucial for us today to understand that the choice to be a worshipper is not a one-time decision; it is an ongoing commitment. If you would ask my wife and me the key to our success as missionaries, we would tell you without hesitation that it was the power of worship. However, we would also readily admit that some days it was difficult to sing or lift our hands because life in Ukraine was hard, and people we encountered could be cruel. It was a choice, and yet oddly, we felt we had no choice. As C.S. Lewis says of his conversion, "I say, 'I chose,' yet it did not really seem possible to do the opposite."[1] It was worship or die on the field of battle. So we chose to worship, just like David.

For most of his life, David had chosen to humble himself and submit himself to God's plan, depending on his provision. There was at least one time in his life, however, when David's hubris overtook him, and he chose to worship himself and his desires rather than God. David was an established king who could have anything he wanted and what he wanted was Bathsheba. As a result, the worshipper became an adulterer and a murderer. For a brief moment, David was blinded to his sin until the prophet Nathan confronted him (2 Sam 12). From the descriptions we have, David was crushed. He was told by Nathan that the sword would not depart from his house, and in fact there was great bloodshed in his family; he was told that God would bring calamity to his house, including sexual sin; and he was told that the son who had been born to Bathsheba would die. The psalm he wrote during this time sounds different from the others because he was pleading with God for mercy:

> Have mercy on me, O God,
> according to your unfailing love;
> according to your great compassion
> blot out my transgressions.
> Wash away all my iniquity
> and cleanse me from my sin.
> For I know my transgressions,
> and my sin is always before me.
> Against you, you only, have I sinned
> and done what is evil in your sight;
> so you are right in your verdict
> and justified when you judge. (Ps 51:1–4)

1. Lewis, *Surprised by Joy*, 224

It's important to note that the choice to worship David had made throughout his life shaped his response to the rock falling on him. He was broken, he probably didn't feel like worshipping, but he knew from experience that this is the thing he needed to do:

> Open my lips, Lord,
> and my mouth will declare your praise.
> You do not delight in sacrifice, or I would bring it;
> you do not take pleasure in burnt offerings.
> My sacrifice, O God, is a broken spirit;
> a broken and contrite heart
> you, God, will not despise. (Ps 51:15–17)

An important lesson from this story is that God can redeem even those whose lives have been crushed. It was from Bathsheba that the heir to the throne, Solomon, came. God can take our disobedience and the evil Satan produces from it and through repentance give us back something good that glorifies him. This is God's miracle in our lives. He did it 3,000 years ago, and he can do it today.

Years later, when David was an old man, he continued to worship God with the perspective of time and trial. In Psalm 37, he observes, " . . . I was young and now I am old . . . " (vs 25), and then goes on:

> The salvation of the righteous comes from the LORD;
> he is their stronghold in time of trouble.
> The LORD helps them and delivers them;
> he delivers them from the wicked and saves them,
> because they take refuge in him. (vss 39–40)

Who would know these things better than David? He was delivered from the lion and the bear as a shepherd, he was delivered from Goliath as a young warrior, he was delivered from Saul over and over again as a seasoned veteran, and he was delivered from prideful sin as an established king. David's life was fueled, filled, and feted by worship. David summed up his lifelong approach to worship in Ps 34:1:

> I will extol the LORD at all times;
>   his praise will always be on my lips.

Can we say the same?

Chapter 7

The Choice for Anointing: The Life of Elisha

MANY TIMES IN THE Bible, those chosen by God for a particular calling or ministry were also anointed. It was a way to call attention to individuals and set them apart, resulting in a change in direction for their lives. The primary biblical references to anointing are in the Old Testament, most often referring to prophets, priests, and kings God had chosen for his service. Nevertheless, because of who we are in Christ, the concept of being anointed still has weight and significance for our lives, precisely because we are now considered to be priests of God. We see this connection in 1 Pet 2:9: "But you are a chosen people, a royal priesthood, a holy nation, God's special possession, that you may declare the praises of him who called you out of darkness into his wonderful light."

What does anointing mean in the context of being set apart by God for ministry? It is not merely being physically anointed with oil. What is our anointing as God's royal priesthood? Simply put, it is the power of the Holy Spirit, the outward expression of God's *boulema* being carried out in the world. The power of the Holy Spirit is a sign to the world of our special relationship with Jesus and the authority we have through his shed blood. First Pet 4:14 says, "If you are insulted because of the name of Christ, you are blessed, for the Spirit of glory and of God rests on you."

We do not have an account of the prophets Elijah or Elisha being anointed for service, though that may have been done.

Despite this, the concept of anointing and the resulting demonstration of the Spirit's power in their lives are undeniable. Anointing for these men took the form of a cloak or mantle that was worn by each of them. The power of anointing to change the course of a life is evident in the story of the call of Elisha by Elijah in 1 Kgs 19:19–21:

> So Elijah went from there and found Elisha son of Shaphat. He was plowing with twelve yoke of oxen, and he himself was driving the twelfth pair. Elijah went up to him and threw his cloak around him. Elisha then left his oxen and ran after Elijah. "Let me kiss my father and mother goodbye," he said, "and then I will come with you."
>
> "Go back," Elijah replied. "What have I done to you?"
>
> So Elisha left him and went back. He took his yoke of oxen and slaughtered them. He burned the plowing equipment to cook the meat and gave it to the people, and they ate. Then he set out to follow Elijah and became his servant.

It's clear that the Lord had prepared Elisha ahead of time for his calling. Perhaps a prophecy had been spoken over him, perhaps the Lord himself had spoken to Elisha. Has the Lord spoken to you about the calling on your life? Have you received a Scripture or prophecy, and now you're waiting to see the fulfillment? Be ready to respond, just like Elisha. When he was called, Elisha quickly said goodbye to his parents, but he did something else significant. He sacrificed the oxen he had been using to plow the field. The oxen represented his old life and the old way of doing things. It has been said that in times of change, we must decide what is dead and must be left behind and what is alive and should be retained. What has God called you to sacrifice? What has he called you to leave behind for the sake of his Kingdom? Are you willing to do what Elisha did?

By sacrificing the oxen, Elisha was saying not only that God was doing a new thing in him, but also that he would not return to his former life. Consider the words of Ps 45:10 and 16:

> Listen, daughter, and pay careful attention:
> Forget your people and your father's house . . .
> Your sons will take the place of your fathers;
> you will make them princes throughout the land.

Meditate on these words: If we forget our fathers, God will give us sons. If we are willing to forget our fathers, which represents our former life, God will give us spiritual sons, a new way of life, a new way of thinking, and a fruitful ministry. This is your inheritance, your anointing.

What is it that God called Elisha to do? Eventually, Elisha would be Elijah's successor. But at first, he was simply a servant to Elijah. Second Kings 3:11 describes Elisha as the man who would pour water on Elijah's hands. Could there be any simpler calling? Elisha's call was to provide Elijah with his basic needs. But what was really going on during this time? Through his service, Elisha was learning what the life of a prophet was all about. He was learning about Elijah's giftings, his heart, and his relationship with God. Every great anointing of God begins with a simple act of obedience. We learn a little, and God teaches us more. We serve a little, and God opens more doors of opportunity to us. We submit to authority, and God gives us greater authority.

And, as often happens, God will test us in our submission to him, to determine the extent of our devotion and perseverance. This happened with Elisha. We read about it in 2 Kgs 2:1–6:

> When the LORD was about to take Elijah up to heaven in a whirlwind, Elijah and Elisha were on their way from Gilgal. Elijah said to Elisha, "Stay here; the LORD has sent me to Bethel."
>
> But Elisha said, "As surely as the LORD lives and as you live, I will not leave you." So they went down to Bethel.
>
> The company of the prophets at Bethel came out to Elisha and asked, "Do you know that the LORD is going to take your master from you today?"
>
> "Yes, I know," Elisha replied, "so be quiet."

> Then Elijah said to him, "Stay here, Elisha; the LORD has sent me to Jericho."
>
> And he replied, "As surely as the LORD lives and as you live, I will not leave you." So they went to Jericho.
>
> The company of the prophets at Jericho went up to Elisha and asked him, "Do you know that the LORD is going to take your master from you today?"
>
> "Yes, I know," he replied, "so be quiet."
>
> Then Elijah said to him, "Stay here; the LORD has sent me to the Jordan."
>
> And he replied, "As surely as the LORD lives and as you live, I will not leave you." So the two of them walked on.

Three times Elijah offers for Elisha to stay behind and become part of the company of the prophets. Have you heard that testing comes in three's? Jesus was tempted three times by Satan in the wilderness. Peter denied knowing Jesus three times before the rooster crowed. And, Jesus required Peter to respond to the question, "Do you love me?" three times following Jesus' resurrection, once for each time Peter denied Jesus. This is a biblical pattern. Each time Elisha was tested, he could have taken the easy way out. He could have moved in with the other prophets of that town and probably had a good life. But for Elisha, this was not enough. He had not given up his old life and spent all that time serving Elijah to miss out on the blessing God had for him. He knew what he wanted, it was in his mind during the whole trip with Elijah, and he would not settle for anything less. Are you willing to settle for something less than God's best? Or, will you stick with God, no matter what, and make the choice for anointing?

There is something very honoring to God about repeated obedience, which often requires great patience. The Bible is full of examples of this kind of obedience: the Israelites marching around Jericho six days, and then seven times on the seventh day; Naaman washing himself seven times in the Jordan River; the disciples waiting ten days in Jerusalem before Pentecost. David says in Ps 63:8:

I cling to you;
    your right hand upholds me.

Are you clinging to God? Is his calling a matter of life and death to you? This is exactly where God wants us.

In 2 Kgs 2:9–10, we understand what it is that Elisha has had in mind the whole time:

> When they had crossed, Elijah said to Elisha, "Tell me, what can I do for you before I am taken from you?"
>
> "Let me inherit a double portion of your spirit," Elisha replied.
>
> "You have asked a difficult thing," Elijah said, "yet if you see me when I am taken from you, it will be yours—otherwise, it will not."

Here we see the connection between anointing and the power of the Spirit. Elisha makes a very bold request. Are you willing to be that bold with God? Elisha had left his former life and his family behind, and he had faithfully served Elijah, probably for years. Then, he had refused to leave Elijah's side during their final journey together. Yet, when Elisha asks for a double portion of Elijah's spirit, Elijah says he has asked for a "difficult thing." Would it really be difficult for God to grant this request? Of course not. What's difficult is bearing the *responsibility* of that calling, the awesome weight of having the Holy Spirit rest *upon* him. This should make us stop and consider. We want God's power in our life, but are we willing to live the life that goes with that anointing? Elisha was willing. Are you willing? Will you boldly ask for God's anointing, as Elisha did?

In 2 Kgs 2:13–14, we see that God granted Elisha's request, and we also see the symbol of the cloak representing the anointing passing from Elijah to Elisha: "Elisha then picked up Elijah's cloak that had fallen from him and went back and stood on the bank of the Jordan. He took the cloak that had fallen from Elijah and struck the water with it. 'Where now is the Lord, the God of Elijah?' he asked. When he struck the water, it divided to the right and to the left, and he crossed over." Elisha sees Elijah's mantle lying on the ground after Elijah was taken up to heaven. He knows it is for him. So, he picks it up and tries it out. Sure enough, he does exactly what Elijah did, he parts the Jordan River. This is a sign to the prophets standing on the other side of the river. Elisha then puts the mantle of Elijah on his own shoulders. Elisha is now literally *wearing* the Spirit. The Spirit is resting *upon* him, and he would go on to do even greater things for the Kingdom of God than Elijah had done.

This same anointing is available today. We have a wonderful promise about this from Jesus himself in John 14:12: "'Very truly I tell you, whoever believes in me will do the works I have been doing, and they will do even greater things than these, because I am going to the Father.'" Jesus said about himself that the Spirit was upon him. Consider what Jesus did while he was on earth and the kind of authority he exercised; to teach, to heal, to set the prisoner free. You will do these works and *more* because of the Spirit who lives inside of you, because of the Spirit who rests *upon* you.

A caution about anointing is given to us by R.T. Kendall in his book *The Anointing*, which I highly recommend. He cites 1 Sam 16:1 and relates it to three kinds of anointing: "The LORD said to Samuel, 'How long will you mourn for Saul, since I have rejected him as king over Israel? Fill your horn with oil and be on your way; I am sending you to Jesse of Bethlehem. I have chosen one of his sons to be king.'" Here we see what Kendall calls past anointing (Saul), present anointing (Samuel), and future anointing (David). Saul was the one who had been considered a prophet at one time, but no longer, and now he was being rejected by God; Samuel was actively conducting God's business, finding the one to anoint; and David was waiting for his turn to be king, which would not take place for many years, and which required great perseverance on David's part. Kendall's point is that we have to be aware where we are in the calling of God for a particular task.

Is it a future anointing, and therefore the best thing we can do is hang in there and not go off half-cocked on some misadventure of our own making? Perhaps you are plowing a field, just working day-to-day. Maybe all you have from God is a promise. This is a good place to be. You're ready for ministry, you're hungry for a fresh touch from God. This is where Elisha was when Elijah found him. He expected a blessing from God, and he was not disappointed. Let me encourage you with the words of 2 Pet 3:9: "God is not slow in keeping his promise . . . " Believe that God has called you and wants to use you mightily for his Kingdom. Learn your lessons, and be ready to obey.

Is it a present anointing, and so we are required to be faithful in that calling, even in the face of opposition? Maybe you are standing today at the Jordan River, and the mantle of the Spirit is lying at your feet. You have an overwhelming desire to pick that mantle up and put it on. God has been preparing you for this moment, and now he asks a simple but profound question: How much do you want that mantle? How much do you want to wear the Spirit? Are you willing to leave everything else behind? Are you willing to live the life of sacrifice that goes with the anointing? I encourage you to say "yes" to God, and then buckle up for the ride of your life.

Or is it a past anointing where, as Kendall illustrates, the tree branch is lying on the ground, but though it is still green, it is no longer alive? An anointing that once characterized your life, where God moved powerfully through you, seems to be on the wane or completely absent today. You go through the motions, doing what you did before, but with less spiritual effect. In that case, you may need to repent. You may have gone your own way in your own power, as Saul did, or you may have lost touch with the Anointed One because of distractions in your life. Whatever the cause, I exhort you to turn back. As Jer 6:16 says in part, " . . . ask where the good way is, and walk in it, and you will find rest for your souls . . . " Our God stands ready to bless you all over again, if you will just ask. And while you're at it, why don't you ask for a double portion?

Chapter 8

The Choice for Suffering: The Life of Paul

THE APOSTLE PAUL HAD a very clear understanding of his calling, which included both positive and negative facets. He knew without a doubt he was called as an apostle, and he began many of his letters to the churches reminding them of that fact. On the other hand, he knew, as Jesus had foretold when Paul was converted, that he would suffer for the Gospel. But this negative aspect of his call was not something he ignored or avoided. Rather, he embraced it, as we read in Acts 21:10–13:

> After we had been there a number of days, a prophet named Agabus came down from Judea. Coming over to us, he took Paul's belt, tied his own hands and feet with it and said, "The Holy Spirit says, 'In this way the Jewish leaders in Jerusalem will bind the owner of this belt and will hand him over to the Gentiles.'" When we heard this, we and the people there pleaded with Paul not to go up to Jerusalem. Then Paul answered, "Why are you weeping and breaking my heart? I am ready not only to be bound, but also to die in Jerusalem for the name of the Lord Jesus."

Likewise, we need to embrace the totality of our call, not just some part of it. When we try to selectively live out our life's work, the way we want to, focusing on the positive and ignoring the negative, we drain our calling of its power, and ultimately do harm to the Kingdom of God.

According to the Bible, brokenness is a sacrifice that is pleasing to God:

> My sacrifice, O God, is a broken spirit;
> a broken and contrite heart
> you, God, will not despise. (Ps 51:17)

We as Christians do not bring animal sacrifices to God because Jesus made the ultimate sacrifice as the Lamb of God. Instead, our Lord expects us to live a life of sacrifice. Who is it Jesus says will be blessed in the Beatitudes? The poor (broken) in spirit, those who mourn, those who are persecuted.

Matthew 21 is a remarkable chapter in the Gospel account of Jesus' life. It begins with his triumphal entry into Jerusalem on Palm Sunday, and it ends with Jesus referring to himself as the cornerstone. In between we see Jesus revealing himself to the crowds, overtly, as the Son of God. Jesus cleanses the temple saying, "' . . . My house will be called a house of prayer . . . '" (vs 13), then he demonstrates his authority over creation by causing a fig tree to wither that was not producing fruit, and finally, he tells two parables which make it clear that God had rejected the leaders of Israel because they had rejected the prophets, John the Baptist, and even the Son of God himself.

Thus, Matt 21:42–43 are a kind of summary of what Jesus has just demonstrated and taught. In these verses, Jesus is warning the spiritual leadership of Israel that their rejection of him would result in the Kingdom of God being given as an inheritance to the Gentiles. But then in verse 44, referring to himself, he says something very strange: "'Anyone who falls on this stone will be broken to pieces; anyone on whom it falls will be crushed.'" Jesus is giving the people a choice between being broken or being crushed. I think if I'd been in the crowd that day, I would have asked him, "Is there another option?" However, despite the verse sounding very negative, it is clear that Jesus considers being crushed to be the worse outcome.

It is not God's desire for his children to be crushed, yet this happens, most often when we *refuse to be broken*. We believe we can choose not to be broken before God and just continue to live our lives. But biblically, if we choose not to be broken, we are also choosing to be crushed. Our God is sovereign. He is all-powerful and in control of every situation. As he says in Isa 46:10, "'My purpose will stand, and I will do all that I please.'" God allows trials in our lives to refine us and purify us. We all have lessons to learn every day about humility and righteousness. If we come before the Lord with acceptable offerings, a broken and contrite spirit, completely dependent on him, releasing control of our lives to him, he will bring healing and victory. If not, we will remain in our circumstances, becoming progressively more desperate, until finally, we are crushed under the weight of the rock.

We fall on the rock, Jesus, in order to die to self. This is to our advantage. The Apostle Paul, who fell on the rock many times, makes the key observation in Col 3:3, "For you have died, and your life is now hidden with Christ in God." If we are dead with regard to the world and our own desires—the lust of the flesh, the pride of life—then Satan is robbed of the weapons he can use against us. Paul also says in Rom 6:7, " . . . anyone who has died has been set free from sin." At the same time, we understand from Scripture that God is close to us in our brokenness, and that we will receive the healing we need. Ps 147:3 assures us that our Lord " . . . heals the brokenhearted and binds up their wounds."

One thing we should also note about suffering is that it is not an unusual thing as far as Scripture is concerned. In fact, it is almost expected. First Peter 4:12–16 states:

> Dear friends, do not be surprised at the fiery ordeal that has come on you to test you, as though something strange were happening to you. But rejoice inasmuch as you participate in the sufferings of Christ, so that you may be overjoyed when his glory is revealed. If you are insulted because of the name of Christ, you are blessed, for the Spirit of glory and of God rests on you. If you suffer, it should not be as a murderer or thief or any other kind of criminal, or even as a meddler. However, if you

> suffer as a Christian, do not be ashamed, but praise God that you bear that name.

Here we see the intermingling of God's *boulema*, his *thelema*, and man's moral will. God's sovereign intent is for his glory to be revealed, God desires that we participate in that glory through suffering for Christ, but it is our choice whether to agree with his *boulema* and *thelema*. Further, not all choices to suffer glorify God. There exists voluntary suffering that is *not* of the kingdom of God, as indicated in these verses—things that we do by habit or out of choice that result in our suffering but which do not glorify God. These are the negative effects of our moral will, things like binging and purging, or cutting, or making bad choices and being involved in destructive relationships. As much as we might feel like these things are not voluntary, they are. It may be, though, the motivation for them lies outside of us, as with the way we were brought up, or traumas we experienced.

Sickness or disease is certainly not voluntary suffering. There are many Christians who believe that God causes sickness to test us or to mature us. Jesus had a different response to this when asked by the disciples about a man born blind (John 9). For the disciples, there were only two possibilities for the cause of the blindness: either the man sinned or his parents sinned. Jesus said it was neither of those things, but rather it had happened "' . . . so that the works of God might be displayed in him'" (John 9:3). So, although sickness is not voluntary, healing from sickness *can* bring glory to God and so can have the same outcome as suffering for Christ. God is in the business of redeeming and restoring, and healing from sickness and disease is part of that restoration.

When we choose to suffer for Christ, it is a redeemed version of suffering because it directly results in glory for God. The church has a rich tradition of this kind of voluntary suffering, one that has been lost in modern western society. We can think of it as intentionally limiting ourselves in some way, usually in terms of our own comfort, to bring about something that's honoring to the Kingdom of God. It may involve risking a friendship or acceptance by family because of our testimony as a Christian; or choosing to fast, or occupying our time with prayer rather than something else; or choosing to live and minister in places that most people would avoid. Paul chose to endure all manner of suffering, as he details in 2 Corinthians 11: imprisonment, beatings, stoning, shipwreck, potential danger both from people and circumstances, sleeplessness, hunger, thirst, and exposure.

Today, we do everything as a society to avoid suffering or loss or deprivation, and we certainly never willingly bring it upon ourselves. This is to our detriment as believers in Jesus Christ. Consider the Beatitudes of Matthew 5 and what and who Jesus calls "blessed": the poor in spirit, those who mourn, and those who are persecuted because of righteousness. Jesus calls us not to avoid these things, but to voluntarily enter into them because there are blessings associated with each. As we read in 1 Pet 4:13, ". . . you participate in the sufferings of Christ, so that you may be overjoyed when his glory is revealed."

We're aware of the imagery in Scripture of the church as the Bride and Jesus as the Bridegroom. Jesus made a key observation in Matt 9:15 about the significance of this relationship as it pertains to voluntary suffering: " . . . 'How can the guests of the bridegroom mourn while he is with them? The time will come when the bridegroom will be taken from them; then they will fast.'" Contrast this with the 1 Peter verse that says we will be overjoyed when Jesus' glory is revealed, that is, when he returns to earth. Simply put, we choose to suffer for the sake of Christ because he is not with us as a way of remembering him while he's gone and as a way of preparing for his return.

In Rev 19:8, we're told that the Bride (us, the Church) will be dressed in clothes that are bright and clean, and that this beautiful wedding dress represents the righteous acts of the saints. We are also told in Rev 21:2 that when the New Jerusalem descends to earth, it is prepared as a bride beautifully dressed for her husband. It is no coincidence that this city is composed of precious stones, pearls and gold, all of which require pressure, irritation or a refining fire to achieve their maximum brilliance and value. This is the Church, prepared for Jesus.

We do not choose to suffer simply to be obedient; rather, we choose to suffer to be prepared, to be ready for the return of the Bridegroom. This is intensely personal and intimate, like an engaged couple making the decision to deny their physical desires and put off getting into bed with each other until they are married. Why do people do that, especially in this day and age? It's not only because it's the right thing to do, or "the Bible tells me so." It is because they believe that what is coming is better than whatever they are denying themselves of in the present. Our voluntary suffering, our denial of our own comfort, is a witness that things are not yet the way God intends. We are expressing longing for restoration and redemption, and in some mysterious way, we are helping to bring about that restoration. We are aligning our moral will with God's *thelema* in order to bring about his *boulema*. This is a very powerful thing, and it was the dynamo that powered the Apostle Paul's life and ministry. Beyond the boldness of his writings, beyond the "go anywhere" mentality of his journeys, he chose not to shrink back from Jesus' terrifying words about him in Acts 9:16: "'I will show him how much he must suffer for my name.'"

The most difficult thing I have to tell you is that sometimes, despite our desire to humble ourselves and be broken and obedient, we are crushed anyway because it is what God has chosen for us to bring himself maximum glory. We have many examples of those who were clearly walking in the *boulema* of God, but who were singled out for crushing: Job, Peter (who Jesus prophesied would be sifted like wheat), Jesus, and of course Paul. In the short-term, each of these crushings could only be viewed as tragedy: Job losing his possessions, his family, his health, and his reputation; Peter denying not only his relationship with Jesus but also everything he had said about Jesus as Messiah and Son of God, essentially throwing away the previous three years of his life; Jesus taking on the scorn and shame of dying a criminal's death; and Paul suffering one setback after another as he gamely attempted to be faithful to his calling.

Seen in isolation these crushings seem unfair and senseless. These individuals did not need to turn from their rebellion. They were each part of God's inner circle, the devout. But in each case, the issue was not simply one of obedience—something much deeper was going on. Somehow, in the cosmic struggle between good and evil, God had decided to stake his claim for the Kingdom on these individuals.

We call God our Redeemer, and so he is. But whereas we think of this as one aspect of his character, I have come to understand that this is in fact *who* he is. He is not like us, trying to figure out how he might redeem a person or situation *after* tragedy has struck, but instead, he is setting the stage for the tragedy, the crushing, in order to *be* the Redeemer. We saw this clearly in God pointing out Job to Satan: "Have you considered my servant Job?" The same was true for Jesus, as prophesied in Isa 53:10, "Yet it was the LORD's will to crush him and cause him to suffer . . . " I believe he did this not only with Job, Peter, Jesus, and Paul, but he does this today with us. We are involved in all-out spiritual warfare. We are the prize *and* the battlefield, as well as the means by which the Kingdom of God is advancing.

At the same time, we know from Ps 34:18:

> The LORD is close to the brokenhearted
> and saves those who are crushed in spirit.

How else could Paul write in Rom 8:18, "I consider that our present sufferings are not worth comparing with the glory that will be revealed in us"?

God may allow the rock to fall on us, but that's not the end of the story. We have a Champion! It is Jesus, who said of himself at the beginning of his ministry that he had been sent to proclaim freedom for the prisoner, recovery of sight for the blind, and release for the oppressed. Jesus makes this offer to you today—he is still the one who can set us free and restore us. Many in Jesus' day rejected him and chose to remain in the prison of their own lives. But, some chose to cry out like blind Bartimeus, "Have mercy on me, Son of David!" And those who were set free and restored by Jesus went on to change the world.

Where are you today? Are your enemies all around you? Then fall on the rock. Choose to be broken before your God. Cry out for his help and his mercy. Don't seek so much to overcome your circumstances as to be purified by them. As Paul wrote out of his own hard-won experience in 2 Cor 4:16–17: "Therefore we do not lose heart. Though outwardly we are wasting away, yet inwardly we are being renewed day by day. For our light and momentary troubles are achieving for us an eternal glory that far outweighs them all."

But perhaps you have chosen to go your own way despite God's warnings in your life. And now the rock has fallen on you. Or perhaps you have been singled out for sifting. Are you crushed today? I have good news for you: The Lord Jesus saves those who are crushed in spirit. That's why he died on the cross 2,000 years ago, that's why he was resurrected on the third day, and that's why he is sitting at the right hand of the Father in heaven interceding for us. Be assured, as a pastor of mine once said, "Your pain has purpose." Choose to be faithful in suffering, but also to look beyond the suffering, as the Apostle Paul did, to the glory produced by that suffering.

Chapter 9

The Choice for Redemption: The Advent of Jesus

As I WRITE THESE words, Christians around the world are celebrating the season of Advent. It is in this season that we anticipate the birth of our Savior Jesus Christ. We do this by preparing ourselves spiritually, but also, we are doing things like buying gifts and cards, making travel plans, cooking and baking (not me, of course, but maybe you), and getting ready to take a break and relax a bit. What I hope to demonstrate in this chapter is that there is no greater example of the transformational nature of choices, God's and ours, than Advent. As we see from Scripture, God's *boulema* and *thelema* are front and center with the birth of Christ, but there is also no getting around the need for and power of a human being who decides to align his or her moral will with God's sovereign plan.

As our central passages, this chapter will focus on the genealogies of Jesus given to us in Matthew 1 and Luke 3. Doesn't that sound exciting? Well, actually, genealogies can be fascinating. Just consider the fact that Ancestry.com has over 4 million subscribers who pay their hard-earned money hoping to understand better their family line and the various influences that shaped them. A few years ago, I happened to find my Dad's old service record from World War II. It occurred to me, as I was leafing through the orders that had assigned him to various duty stations around the world that records and genealogies like that are a kind of movie of a person's life. We begin to understand what predisposed them to do what they did and ultimately what motivates us today.

What is most striking for me when I look at these records is the seemingly unplanned events in our lives and our family lines that produced us—chance meetings, random circumstances that threw people together, illnesses and deaths that rerouted family trees, the influence of wars, etc. We all have these stories, and because Jesus came in human form at the Nativity, he also has these stories.

The Apostle Paul encouraged Timothy not to allow people to argue about genealogies, so I will not dwell on the difficult aspects of the genealogies presented to us in Matthew 1 and Luke 3. Rather, I will talk about what is generally accepted about them, as well as the people included in them, as a way of talking about how far God went to have his *boulema* realized.

The two genealogies are very different from each other, and there is a good reason for that: They were intended for completely different audiences. Matthew was writing to Jewish Christians, and Luke was writing to Gentile Christians. The faith of each kind of reader would be strengthened by particular kinds of information about Jesus. Matthew announces the intent of his genealogy in the first verse of his gospel:

> This is the genealogy of Jesus the Messiah the son of David, the son of Abraham (Matt 1:1)

Matthew's intention was to establish the succession of Jesus to the throne of David, as well as the Jewishness of Jesus as a child of Abraham. Thus, he begins with Abraham and traces Jesus' family tree through the royal line of David and ultimately to Jesus. Note especially that in this genealogy, which is understood to be through Joseph's side of the family, it says that David was the father of Solomon. Actually, David had many sons, but only one of them became king after him, and that was Solomon. Note also in this genealogy the inclusion of women's names, which was highly unusual for the time, but which is very significant in understanding Jesus' story. We will look at this more closely in a moment.

Now you may think to yourself, yes, but Joseph wasn't Jesus' biological father. True, but as we will see, there was a blood connection between Jesus and David and therefore the royal line. What Matthew is alluding to is the promise David received from God that he would never fail to have an heir on the throne: "'Your house and your kingdom will endure forever before me; your throne will be established forever'" (2 Sam 7:16). Matthew's genealogy is about authority rather than blood. Joseph carried the family name of the kings of Israel, and this is what Jesus inherited from him.

This stands in contrast to the genealogy presented by Luke. For many reasons, this heredity is understood to be Mary's side of the family, the bloodline. This is the reason for the differences in the father of Joseph between the genealogies. It is assumed that Mary's father had no sons, and so according to Jewish custom the son-in-law became the son and the heir. But the genealogies of Matthew and Luke also differ in very significant ways because of the intended audiences.

The Gentile Christians would not have cared about Jesus' royal connections. Instead, they cared about their own connection to God through Jesus—that they had been grafted into the vine and now were considered to be on an equal footing with the Jews as God's chosen people. Thus, Luke's genealogy begins with Jesus and traces his roots all the way *back* to the first man, Adam, and ultimately to God.

We also see that Luke did not begin his gospel with the genealogy like Matthew, but chose to sandwich it in between the story of Jesus' baptism in the Jordan and his temptation in the wilderness. This is yet another way that Luke places the emphasis on Jesus as the Son of God. At the Jordan, God the Father says, "You are my Son" (Luke 3:22), and in the wilderness Satan begins his temptations of Jesus with the words, "If you are the son of God . . . " (Luke 4:3). The genealogy affirms both of these statements.

The crucial correspondence of the two genealogies is that they both arrive at David and trace their way back to Judah. This is the basis for the title given to Jesus in Rev 5:5 where it says, "Then one of the elders said to me, 'Do not weep! See, the Lion of the tribe of Judah, the Root of David, has triumphed . . . '" This connection became part of Jesus' identity exactly because it was part of his parents' identity. And it is precisely for this reason that Joseph and Mary had to make the hazardous trip from Nazareth to Bethlehem when Mary was about to give birth. According to Luke, they had to go to Judea (Judah), to the city of David (Bethlehem) to be counted as part of the census ordered by the Roman Caesar at that time.

Consider the confluence of events required to bring all of this together at the moment of Jesus' birth: both sides of the family tracing their line back to David and Judah, Joseph and Mary engaged to be married, Mary becoming pregnant by the Holy Spirit, Caesar Augustus choosing that exact time to conduct the census. It boggles the mind.

But that's only the beginning of what the genealogies of Jesus teach us about God's preparation for his birth. As I mentioned before, a unique aspect of Matthew's genealogy is the inclusion of women's names, which was highly unusual for the time, but which I think was meant to instruct us further about the extent to which God was willing to go to bring about the Nativity. Matthew specifically mentions Tamar, Rahab, Ruth and Uriah's wife, who we know was Bathsheba. If you don't know anything about the Old Testament, these names may not mean much to you, but each is filled with meaning and significance. We'll just consider each one briefly, in light of God's preparation for Jesus' advent.

We know that at least two of these women were Gentiles, and it's possible that all four of the women were, which is another remarkable thing about their inclusion in the genealogy. But even if they weren't all Gentiles, one thing we can say for sure about all the women in Matthew 1 is that their moral will was very strong, and at crucial moments in history they acted decisively. Perhaps you've seen the bumper sticker that says, "Well-behaved women rarely make history." The lives of these four women could have been tragic were it not for God's *thelema* to redeem them, which may be the very reason they are included in the Great Redeemer's genealogy.

> Judah the father of Perez and Zerah, whose mother was Tamar . . . (Matt 1:3)

Tamar literally rescued Judah's family from obscurity through a very bold maneuver on her part which you can read about in Genesis 38. As a result of her action, her son Perez became an ancestor of King David.

> Salmon the father of Boaz, whose mother was Rahab . . . (Matt 1:5)

Rahab was the informant who made the decision to protect her family line (and, it turned out, Jesus' as well) by harboring spies who were collecting intelligence on Jericho for an invasion by the Israelites; you can read about that in Joshua 2. Rahab is one of only two women mentioned by name in the hall of faith given to us in Hebrews 11.

> . . . Boaz the father of Obed, whose mother was Ruth . . . (Matt 1:5)

Ruth was a widow, like Tamar, who decided to stay with her mother-in-law Naomi after both of their husbands had died. Ruth left her home country, her family, and everything she knew, and they both came to Bethlehem where Ruth met and married Boaz. As a result, Ruth became the great grandmother of King David and an ancestor of Jesus. This connection to Bethlehem was the reason Joseph and Mary had to make their journey for the census. There are only two books of the Bible named for women, and Ruth's book is one of them.

> . . . David was the father of Solomon, whose mother had been Uriah's wife (Matt 1:6)

Uriah's wife, Bathsheba, was a potentially tragic figure, the woman who King David had an adulterous affair with, whose husband David subsequently had murdered, and who lost her first child shortly after its birth. But God redeemed this tragedy, making her the mother of Solomon, who would take the throne after David's death. Except for Jesus' death and resurrection, there may be no greater story of redemption in the Bible; you can read about that in 2 Samuel 11 and 12.

I want to dwell for a moment more on Ruth because God's preparation for the Nativity actually extends through Ruth all the way back to the giving of the Law to Moses and the Israelites. How was it that Ruth, a Gentile, was included in Jesus' line? Ironically, it was because of the Law established by God for the Jewish people. It was specifically forbidden in the Law for the Israelites, the people of promise, to mistreat or take advantage of foreigners. Further, the Israelites were expected to share some of their harvest with non-Jews. "'When you reap the harvest of your land, do not reap to the very edges of your field or gather the gleanings of your harvest. Leave them for the poor and for the foreigner residing among you. I am the LORD your God'" (Lev 23:22). We see this principle at work in the Book of Ruth: This is how Ruth, a foreigner, survived when she and her mother-in-law returned to Israel, and it is also how Ruth met Boaz, the owner of a field, and became an ancestor of both David and Jesus.

Do the preparations go back farther than the Law? Jesus was part of the chosen race of Israel, and both of the genealogies trace Jesus' line back through Judah to Jacob, Isaac, and Abraham. This was Jesus' natural heritage. His *spiritual* lineage goes through someone named Melchizedek, an intriguing figure introduced to us in Genesis who is not included in either genealogy, but who the writer of Hebrews ties directly to Jesus. Twice the author quotes a verse from Ps 110, " . . . You are a priest forever, in the order of Melchizedek" (Heb 5:6, 7:17).

Just as Jesus is to reign on David's throne forever, he is also to be our priest forever, making intercession to the Father on our behalf. But, who was Melchizedek? He only makes a cameo appearance in Gen 14:18–20:

> Then Melchizedek king of Salem brought out bread and wine. He was priest of God Most High, and he blessed Abram, saying,

"Blessed be Abram by God Most High,
  Creator of heaven and earth.
And praise be to God Most High,
  who delivered your enemies into your hand."
Then Abram gave him a tenth of everything.

So, this King of Salem (Jerusalem) was also a priest, though this event preceded the giving of the Law and the creation of the office of priest. Melchizedek offers Abram bread and wine, similar to Jesus giving the bread and wine to the disciples at the last supper, a tradition we carry on through communion. He blesses Abram with a blessing from God, and Abram gives him a tithe. All of these symbols and actions foreshadowed the Law and found their fulfillment in the One who completed the Law, Jesus.

But, that's not where Luke's genealogy ends. It traces Jesus' line back to Adam, the first man. Is there more than just a natural connection? Of course, the Garden of Eden is where humans fell and sin entered the world. But it's also where we lost the spiritual authority we had been given by God at creation. In Genesis 3 we have the story of the fall and God's pronouncement about how the world would work after that time. Interestingly, in the process of cursing the snake, who was the tempter and who we understand to be Satan, we see the first allusion to Jesus in the Bible, establishing the tension that would play itself out during Jesus' life and into our own time:

So the Lord God said to the serpent, "Because you have done this,

"Cursed are you above all livestock
  and all wild animals!
You will crawl on your belly
  and you will eat dust
  all the days of your life.
And I will put enmity
  between you and the woman,
  and between your offspring and hers;

he will crush your head,
and you will strike his heel." (Gen 3:14–15)

So, in the midst of the tragedy of the fall, God was preparing for Jesus' advent, establishing the spiritual conflict between Jesus and Satan that would play itself out in Jesus' life and in the 2000 plus years that have followed. But Adam is not the end of the line in Luke's genealogy; that place is reserved for God. There is an aspect of the eternal to this record, not only going forward, but also looking back. Somehow, mysteriously, Jesus' birth was planned even before the events that took place in the Garden. Second Tim 1:9–10 says: "He has saved us and called us to a holy life—not because of anything we have done but because of his own purpose and grace. This grace was given us in Christ Jesus *before the beginning of time*, but it has now been revealed through the appearing of our Savior, Christ Jesus, who has destroyed death and has brought life and immortality to light through the gospel" (emphasis added).

Whether we are preparing for Christmas or preparing to go on a family trip, we need to remind ourselves that we can't out-prepare God. All his preparations were for us, for this moment, right here, right now. This isn't some white elephant gift exchange where God looked around heaven and said, "What can I give that I don't really need anymore?" It isn't even like Santa Claus reaching into his bag and pulling out something nice from a whole bunch of different gifts. There was only *one choice* of a gift for God the Father to give us, and that was Jesus, the incarnation of God's *boulema* and *thelema.* And he sent the gift of his Son through generation after generation of sometimes inspirational but always flawed human beings because he wanted to make sure we understood that our choices matter to him.

Conclusion

HAVING READ THE PRECEDING pages, what do you think of my thesis from the Introduction? I said that I believe the highest *boulema* is God's purpose to bring about maximum glory for himself, the purest *thelema* is God's desire to bless and protect his people, and the most powerful moral will is our agreement with God's *boulema* and *thelema*. How does this square with what you have read? Perhaps more importantly, is the premise borne out in your own experience? It should be obvious by now that these considerations are not just theoretical exercises for me, and I hope you know that it is not my intention to preach at you with the challenging lives of those profiled in the previous chapters. For me, these biblical characters are still alive because the decisions they had to make resonate with my own life and choices today. We are handicapped in our reading of the Bible because we know how the story turns out. As a result, scriptural stories can seem artificial and detached from reality. I have tried to paint the individuals presented in this book as those who didn't know how their story would end and who had to make choices anyway, much as we have to every day. I am grateful for their examples, especially because the biblical narratives combine the heroic model of doing the right thing at the right time for the right reason with honest pictures of human weakness, fallibility, and questioning.

How have God's choices influenced your own life? How have your choices been either in concert with God's choices or caused you to miss out on his offers of blessing? Whose experience among those profiled in the previous chapters do you most identify with? Whose life do you desire to emulate? We all need role models, and certainly these are not the only ones available to us. Not only are there many other inspiring biblical characters we can name, but there are also men and women of faith who have lived more recently, or perhaps are living now, after whom we might model our choices. But make no mistake, no matter how we go about it, we must make choices, and our choices matter. It's all about choices.

Bibliography

Adichie, C.N. *The Danger of a Single Story*. Video. 2009. Retrieved from https://www.ted.com/talks/chimamanda_adichie_the_danger_of_a_single_story/transcript.

Butler, D.J. *I Will Change Your Name*. Song. 1987. Mercy/Vineyard.

Kendall, R.T. *The Anointing: Yesterday, Today, Tomorrow*. Nashville: Thomas Nelson, 1999.

Knortz, J.A. *The Strategic Leadership of Admiral Chester W. Nimitz*. United States Army War College, 2012. Retrieved from http://www.dtic.mil/dtic/tr/fulltext/u2/a561569.pdf.

Lewis, C.S. *Surprised by Joy: The Shape of My Early Life*. New York: Harcourt, Brace & World, 1955.

Peterson, Eugene. *A Long Obedience in the Same Direction: Discipleship in an Instant Society*. Downers Grove, IL: InterVarsity, 2000.

Stott, J.R.W. "The Living God is a Missionary God." In *Perspectives on the World Christian Movement: A Reader*, 3rd ed. edited by Ralph D. Winter et al., 3-9. Pasadena, CA: William Carey Library, 1999.

Woodward, J.R. *Creating a Missional Culture: Equipping the Church for the Sake of the World*. Downers Grove, IL: InterVarsity, 2012.

Yancey, Philip. *Disappointment with God*. Grand Rapids, MI: Zondervan, 1988.

www.ingramcontent.com/pod-product-compliance
Lightning Source LLC
Chambersburg PA
CBHW071104090426
42737CB00013B/2476